CW00631380

THE THINGS YOU SEE...

A collection of stories by

Philip Whiteland

The Things You See...

Published by Philip Whiteland

This print edition published 2018

Also available as Kindle editions by this author:

Steady Past Your Granny's

Crutches for Ducks

A Kick at the Pantry Door

Giving a Bull Strawberries

A Christmas Cracker

Cover design: John Steele

Cover photo: Hilary Whiteland

Cover Photo: *Philip leaning on another example of Burton's street art.   This time it is a concrete facsimile of the iconic jar of a well-known vegetable extract which is synonymous with Burton upon Trent.   At least it's more relevant than a 30 foot high stainless steel shovel! (see Giving a Bull Strawberries)*

Dedicated to the very patient readers of the Derby Telegraph's Bygones page over the years and to Jane Goddard, the kind, supportive and encouraging editor of that page, without whom a lot of this book would never have happened - so now you know who to blame!

CONTENTS

INTRODUCTION

I think this is the bit that scares me the most about putting these collections of stories together. What do you say, at this point, which will persuade the not 100% committed reader to plough on and find out what the book is all about?

I suppose I could mention the structure of the book, which is based on that chocolate bar which used to promise to help you to 'work, rest and play'. Do you remember those? When they first came out it took strong men to lift them from the counter and they seemed to be the calorific equivalent of a three-course dinner. Today, it seems as if they're gone in one bite. Speaking of which, what the heck is 'fun' about 'fun-sized' chocolate bars? It's just another way of saying 'miniscule' and making it sound like something to aspire to, which I don't in any context.

Where was I? I'm sorry, this happens a lot these days. There I am, happily pursuing a theme when I suddenly realise I've no idea what I was trying to do. I actually had to give up at a 'Pay at Pump' petrol pump the other day because I had completely lost the plot as to how to make it work. I finished up driving out and driving back in again so that I could pay at the kiosk. It's all rather sad, really, isn't it? Oh, yes, I remember, the structure of this book! Well, I thought if 'work, rest and play' are good enough for them, then they're good enough for me. Therefore, in this book you'll find:

In '**Work**' I join the ranks of the employed at the beginning of the 1970s, firstly as an inept packer of plastics before moving to 'a nice dry job with no heavy lifting' in a dark, satanic paper mill. We learn about my struggles with punctuality, the difficulties of working in the darkness of the 3-Day-Week and why I had real reason to be grateful for Ted Heath.

'**Play**' brings tales of a boozy holiday in Franco's Majorca in the 1970s, a fleeting role in a 'Look at Life' documentary, Cilla Black, Soap Operas, an insight into the Cultural Quarter of Stoke-on-Trent and some tales from a trip to Australia.

Finally, 'the **Rest**' shovels up everything that wouldn't fit into the first two, including a tour around a pub in the 1960s, getting a brace fitted at the dentist's, difficulties with sanitary arrangements, why grass should be left alone, why shopping with your wife is an overrated pastime, a grumble about grammar and why it is absolutely fine to be a NIMBY. All wrapped up with the Title article, which is not for the faint-hearted.

Oh, and there are some '**Mis-shapes**' at the end, which you might enjoy.

Why the title - 'The Things You See...'? Well, it's another one of those phrases my parents trotted out on a regular basis. In full, it should read "The things you see, when you haven't got a gun", which has nothing to do with shooting anything but was usually applied when one or other of them spotted somebody they thought looked ridiculous or outrageous. I thought it fitted quite well with a whole variety of things you'll see as you meander through this book, particularly in the title article. If all else fails, it should endear me to the National Rifle Association in the U.S. and the Countryside Alliance in the U.K. You have to take your readers where you can get them, these days ;-)

WORK

Plastic People

'A' Level Playing Field

In September, 2015, my four-year-old grandson started Primary School, and seems to have taken to it considerably more cheerfully than I did at his age. Partly because he has been a member of the local Pre-School Playgroup since he was just over two years old, so I suppose it just seems like more of the same.

Regular readers will recall that I was nowhere near as sanguine back in 1959. I think I was ok for the first couple of weeks, but then it dawned on me that this was something I was stuck with for at least the next 11 years. I decided I didn't want to play anymore and had to be dragged, kicking and screaming, from our house in Anglesey Road to Uxbridge Street Infants yelling throughout *"I don't want to go to school, I don't mind being a dunce"* (which was the dread outcome that my mum had threatened me with if I didn't attend.)

Part of the problem was that I didn't really like children *en masse,* largely because I had never had to deal with more than one at a time before. Dumped in at the deep end, with hordes of them screaming and shouting, after five years of relative tranquillity and peaceful play, seemed a bit much to me. Therefore, despite all the talk about 'the good old days', I think our approach to pre-school preparation now is a lot more effective, and better informed, than it was in my childhood.

Inevitably, the 11 years passed and, although I can hardly say they were the best years of my life, something must have gone right as I signed on for a further two at Burton Technical College. Unfortunately, freed from the constraints of the school system (my five-year-old self would have been delighted) I'm afraid that I didn't apply myself as diligently as I should have done. I was 'called to the bar' at an early stage and, as a consequence, quite a number of mornings didn't happen until lunchtime.

At the end of the two year stretch, I began looking for gainful employment. This was during one of those periods when the newspapers were full of dire warnings about the difficulty of getting a job, any job. It was in this frame of mind that I spotted an advertisement in the local paper for a Warehouseman/Clerk vacancy at a local DIY Plastics warehouse. This sounded like my sort of thing as it seemed to fulfil my desire for a 'nice dry job with no heavy lifting' (I had focused on the 'clerk' element of the job title and ignored the 'warehouseman' bit.) In addition, it was in Anglesey Road and was only a matter of minutes from where I lived.

The advert gave a number to ring, so I hurried to the nearest telephone kiosk with my best mate, Kev, in tow (he had left college a year earlier and was 'between occupations'). My call was answered by a woman with the sexiest telephone voice I had ever heard. Now, the only thing about me that I was reasonably pleased with was my voice, so we appeared to hit it off on the 'phone. She told me to come down straight away for an interview, and Kev and I hurried to see what this temptress looked like in person.

I think we were a bit of a disappointment to each other, in all honesty, but I left Kev chatting to her (he was always popular with the ladies) whilst I had an interview with one of the directors. To my surprise, my prospective 'A' levels were a problem, he thought these indicated that I was over-qualified (I was) and would leave within weeks (I didn't). Therefore I had to spend a good deal of time down-playing my qualifications and insisting that packing plastic products was exactly what my education had been leading to.

I don't suppose he believed me but he gave me the job anyway. However, I had to start the following Monday and I hadn't yet officially left College, which proved to be a bit of a problem.

Packing Up School

You would have thought that the educational establishment would have been only too happy to wave goodbye to the reluctant pupil who had to be dragged, kicking and screaming, to school some thirteen years earlier. However, they weren't quite finished with me yet. I had three more weeks to serve at Burton Technical College.

I wrote to the Principal, asking politely if they could manage without my continued presence, which I thought would be no problem as all exams had been completed and there was no real reason for any further attendance. Whether I caught him on a bad day, I don't know, but he called me in to his office and informed me, in no uncertain manner, that I could not be released and would have to serve my full term. I suppose he was less than pleased that two years of 'A' level study had led to my obtaining a job packing plastics, but I took the view that beggars can't be choosers and I would rather be in employment, any employment, than propping up the walls of the Job Centre.

My prospective employers, who I'll call Midland Area Plastics, were less than impressed at the delay but sportingly agreed to wait another three weeks for me to join them.

I mentioned earlier that I had focused more on the 'clerk' element of the job title than the 'packer' bit, when I applied, and I think I therefore had a somewhat confused idea about what I would be doing. A sign of my confusion was that I turned up, on the first day, dressed in an old sports jacket and shirt of my dad's but with the addition of a knitted tie. I think I was trying to cover all possibilities, clearly without success.

Midland Area Plastics (MAP) had been established to take advantage of the great British D.I.Y. boom. Although B & Q had commenced operations in 1969 (soon to be followed by many other D.I.Y. retail warehouses) in 1972, when I started work, Britain was still a nation of hardware shops and small D.I.Y. outlets and it was primarily these that formed MAP's customer base.

As a new start-up company, MAP had set up shop in one of a series of old warehouses on Anglesey Road, which had been sublet into many different units. Entering from the front, the visitor was confronted with a flight of stairs up to the relatively modern offices. However, if you continued straight on, past the stairs, you entered the gloom of an ancient warehouse, with racks of shelving on either side, and eight huge wooden benches, much scarred and worn by years of use, which constituted the packing stations. I was assigned one of these benches and Pete, the leading hand, began to show me the ropes.

The Front Entrance to the Plastics Warehouse as it is now

The 1970s marked the beginnings of a trend in which everything that had previously been made of wood, was replaced with plastic equivalents. Therefore, the racks of shelves contained a variety of 6' and 8' lengths of plastic, some curved or angled to provide edging, some more like thin planks of wood and some piano-hinged. All were available in white, black or wood-effect. In addition, there were rolls of metal-effect wallpaper and self-adhesive edging strips. Everything that the D.I.Y. enthusiast needed to turn his/her home into a plastic palace. You may recall that the 1970s were the decade that taste forgot? Well, it started here.

The first thing I discovered was that virtually every one of the packing team smoked. Moreover, there was a convention that, if one lit a cigarette he had to give one to all of the rest of the team ('crashing the ash' as it was termed). This, inevitably, meant that we were all smoking at the rate of the most addicted amongst us. I went from 5 a day to 40 a day within the first week!

Weighing The Job Up!

There are a number of things that strike you when you first start work. The first is that you're never again going to have as many holidays as you had when you were at school/college. That comes as a bit of a blow, unless, of course, you happen to be going to work in a school or college. The second is that days start rather earlier, and finish rather later, than they used to. Thirdly, there's an awful lot of standing around, lifting and carrying involved.

By the end of the first day, I was completely shattered! I had never worked so hard in my life, and yet I had been given a relatively easy day to get me used to everything that was involved.

Pete, the supervisor, showed me the ropes (or rather, the string, as it turned out). Firstly, you had to take an order form from the tray. The rule was that you had to take the top one and not 'cherry pick' an easier one from underneath. Because I was training, I was allowed to have a few simple ones to begin with.

It was then a matter of collecting the relevant plastic items from the shelving, ideally 'picking' lengths of plastic of the same length to make up one parcel, then forming the various lengths of plastic into a roughly square shaped stack for ease of packing. A piece of corrugated cardboard would be cut for each end of the stack of plastic, to protect the ends of the lengths. Next, the stack had to be wrapped in corrugated cardboard. There was a 6' high roll of this by each packing station, along with a 3' high roll for smaller parcels. Most parcels took two lengths of the larger roll, overlapped and folded over at each end, to completely cover the plastic inside.

Now came the tricky bit. The cardboard had to be secured by means of string, at various points along the parcel. Pete showed me how to do this using a particular knot that had been adopted for the purpose. Having formed the knot, you then had to pull the string as tight as possible around the parcel, giving it a good yank to hold it in place. This, unfortunately, had the unhappy effect of driving the string into the side of your hand like a cheese-wire. Not a problem for those who had worked here for a while and whose hands were hardened to this, but for me it was excruciatingly painful and my right hand was a bloody mess by the end of the day.

You may remember that the job had been described as a Warehouse Clerk/Packer and I had rather pinned my hopes on the clerical element? Well, the only clerical aspect I could find was the filling out of the address labels at the end of the packing process. At least this gave the opportunity for a brief sit down on the smaller of the rolls of cardboard.

With the parcels now wrapped and labelled, they had to be weighed and entered into the despatch book for the distribution company to collect at the end of the day. You've heard of companies having economies of scale? Well this one had achieved a major economy by not having any scales at all! Pete helped me to estimate my first attempts, but then I was on my own. The weights had to be recorded in hundredweights, quarters and pounds, and, inevitably you had to vary the recorded weights a bit so that they didn't look too neat and artificial.

Finally, the parcels were carefully stacked by the back door, ready for the arrival of the lorry later. Woe betide anyone whose slipshod stacking caused the whole lot to slide, like an avalanche, to the floor, as I did more than once.

I often wonder if the distribution company had any idea that the recorded weights were basically a work of fiction!

Christmas Boxes

The lack of holidays once you start work is never more evident than at Christmas. Gone are the halcyon days when you had at least three weeks in which to slump on the settee, eating tins of sweets and watching old movies. Suddenly you find that Christmas consists of Christmas Day and Boxing Day, if you're lucky!

I wasn't at all sure what to expect from my first Christmas at the plastics warehouse, having never had a Christmas at work before. More to the point, I wasn't expecting very much at all, as our employers were hardly renowned for their generosity. It was the only place I have ever worked where overtime, during the week and on Saturday mornings, was paid at time and a fifth. I think it jumped up to time and a quarter on a Saturday afternoon and reached the heady heights of time and a half on a Sunday. So you'll appreciate that no-one had any great hopes for the festive season.

Nevertheless, on our last working day before Christmas, we were invited up to the staff room for a drink with the Directors. My recollection of this event is somewhat hazy, for reasons that will become apparent, but I do recall that, with all of us up there at the same time, there were insufficient seats, so many of us had to sit cross-legged on the floor and propped against the wall.

The 'drink' turned out to be neat whisky, with no alternatives or additives. I'm not a great fan of whisky at any time of the day, and particularly not in the morning, but I've also never knowingly turned down the chance of a free drink. As I always fought a losing battle between getting up sufficiently early to have breakfast, and staying in bed for five minutes longer, there was nothing in my digestive system to act as a barrier to the sudden influx of spirits. From a look around the room, it became clear that a number of my colleagues were in the same boat.

I think some mince pies were going around too. I have since discovered that this is always the case, wherever you work. Mince pies have been a source of competition, between those who wish to demonstrate their baking skills, since long before Mary Berry and Paul Hollywood were high enough to turn the oven on.

There were Christmas songs playing in the background and we were all getting distinctly merrier and unfit for further work. One of the girls decided to bestow Christmas kisses on us all, and these became decidedly more amorous as the morning progressed.

Eventually, the Directors announced that work had finished for the day (which was a wise decision, under the circumstances) and we could all go home. Before we headed off, however, we were given our Christmas Box, which turned out to be a bottle of whisky each. This was a pretty generous present in the early 1970s, as spirits were quite expensive and reserved for high days and holidays.

We made our unsteady way back down to the warehouse to collect our belongings and then to fetch our bikes from outside (most of us arrived by pedal power). I had an additional burden because I had been conned into buying a boxed set of classical LPs from one of my workmates. This was largely my own fault for trying to adopt an image of intellectual superiority and musical discernment which was at odds with reality. I now had to get this box of LPs, and a bottle of whisky, home on my bike, whilst being definitely unfit to even walk with it. It is a sad indictment of my sense of priorities that I managed to get home with the whisky intact but the box of LPs somewhat battered and bruised.

I did do better than one of mates, however, who dropped his bottle as he tried to get on his bike. There is no sadder sight than that of someone valiantly trying to retrieve the precious liquid from the tarmac, with the aid of a handkerchief, and transferring it back into the broken shards of glass.

He didn't succeed.

Battle of the Bands

One of the biggest problems with work, when you first enter employment, is that, by and large...it's boring!

It doesn't matter how well educated or well qualified you might be, your initial tasks are bound to be pretty mundane and repetitive. This takes some getting used to, after a lifetime spent in an educational environment which aims, for the most part, to try and capture your attention and interest in challenging ways. This is particularly true if your chosen occupation involves packing plastic items for delivery to the DIY trade.

There were various opportunities to break the monotony, some of which arose as part of the work and others which didn't, like our regular elastic band wars. These would start fairly innocuously. An errant elastic band would fly over the packing benches and strike someone. Inevitably there would be a reply in kind and, within seconds, the whole packing team would be flicking elastic bands at each other with increasing ferocity. At their best, these sessions took on the appearance of a Wild West shoot-out with people hunkered down behind rolls of corrugated cardboard, only emerging to make a sly shot at one of 'the enemy'. Of course, these battles were only possible if the

Warehouse Manager was either missing, or otherwise occupied. If he made a sudden reappearance, we had to resume our duties and tidy up the 'spent ammunition' pretty quickly.

Deliveries from our suppliers were another source of variety in our working lives. As we had no manual handling equipment of any sort, these had to be off-loaded by hand. One delivery I always used to dread was that of the metal coated, self-adhesive wallpaper. If you're wondering who, in their right mind, would want metal coated, self-adhesive wallpaper, you have to remember that this was the 1970's.

To offload this item, we formed a 'human chain' between the lorry and the requisite shelving and threw the wallpaper rolls from one to another. In every all-male team there is bound to be one who fancies himself as a 'hard case' and, for this role, we had Ralph (name changed to protect the guilty). Ralph used to demonstrate his superiority over the rest of us, on a day-to-day basis, by constructing packages of immense weight. Vast amounts of plastic, which most of us would have shared between two or three parcels, Ralph formed into gigantic creations weighing several hundredweight. No-one else could even lift these, let alone load them onto the lorry at the end of the day.

For the wallpaper delivery, Ralph always rushed to position himself at the head of the chain, so that he was the first one to receive the rolls from the lorry. Normal wallpaper rolls are reasonably heavy and metal-coated ones are considerably more so. His delight was in throwing each roll as hard and fast as possible at the next man in the chain, with the ambition of, at least, forcing him to drop it and, at best, causing physical injury. If he didn't get you with the first roll, then the force, speed and pace of delivery all increased until the inevitable happened. At this point, our Team Leader would usually take over the position of the injured party and dare Ralph to try it on with him.

The rear loading bay of the plastics warehouse (as it is today)

Ralph's desire to prove his superiority did come into its own, however, whenever we had a delivery which had to be stored on the top floor. To do this, we had a block and tackle arrangement in which the plastic was tied to a rope and then the majority of the team would run across the top floor, holding the rope, and haul the load up to the doorway. At this point, Ralph, with one hand holding on to the door frame, would swing out into thin air and grab the load to guide it into the warehouse. I think we were all quite happy for him to prove his worth in this way.

You may have gathered that all of this took place well before the Health and Safety at Work Act!

Working with Wogan

The constant background to our labours was the radio. From dawn till dusk, and certainly every working hour, the portable radio positioned in the centre of our group of workbenches filled the warehouse with non-stop Radio 1 (this being the only radio station available that we all liked). I had an insatiable interest in contemporary music, even in the 1970s, an era which might well have fulfilled the Don McLean definition of 'the day the music died'. I also enjoyed the whole gamut of Radio 1 presenters, such as Tony Blackburn, Dave Lee Travis, Noel Edmonds and so on. In those days, of course, the DJ was very much the star of the show, because there were so few of them and they were a relatively new concept. As a consequence, a number of them developed star-sized egos!

I'm willing to be shot down in flames, but I'm fairly sure that there were still chunks of the day when Radios 1 and 2 joined forces, which accounted for the presence of such unlikely Radio 1 voices as Jimmy Young, Pete Murray and, of course, the incomparable Terry Wogan.

By Julie anne Johnson from Cheltenham, UK (Terry Wogan°○●○•°) [CC BY 2.0 (http://creativecommons.org/licenses/by/2.0)], via Wikimedia Commons

Listening to the Terry Wogan show was the highlight of my day and, if you will bear with me, I would like to go slightly off topic to remember him.

I loved his sly humour and the choice of music, which was slightly less Top 40 obsessed than his contemporaries. I remember that he championed the music of Peter Skellern, which I came to love, but which was hardly typical Radio 1 material. I think I loved Terry's programmes then because he wasn't trying to be a sort of watered-down American (unlike most of the Radio 1 presenters) and he was considerably less frenetic. He didn't take himself too seriously either, which was a notable failing in many of the early radio presenters, who often came to believe in their own publicity.

When he moved to the Breakfast show, I enjoyed listening to him as I was getting ready to go to work, and I often found my mum in a helpless state of 'the giggles' at something he'd said. Waking up to Wogan was very much a key part of our day.

When he decided to leave radio to further his television career, in 1984, I was bereft. I wondered whether he was making the right choice as, in my eyes, he was incomparable on the radio but rather average on television. In fact, some years later when I was undertaking a recruitment and selection module, the tutor advised us to observe Terry's television chat show as a prime example of how *not* to conduct interviews, which was perhaps a bit harsh but not a million miles from the truth.

I remember listening with glee to his first radio show when he returned to the Breakfast slot in 1993 and being somewhat concerned that the smooth operation and effortless wit was not quite there. I needn't have worried, as he was back to his usual excellence within a few days and stayed that way for the rest of his radio career. Only a supreme professional would have entrusted his radio 'script' to his listeners and have dared to grace the airways with the 'Janet and John' stories.

From 1990 to 1995 I had a bash at presenting on Hospital Radio and I suppose I had Terry in mind as my role model. The one thing it did bring home to me was just how difficult it is to present a radio show with the ease with which he seemed to do it. You can only achieve this if you have supreme talent, an incredibly lively and energetic mind, and a warmth that somehow transmits itself through the broadcasting medium, all of which he had in bucket-loads.

I very much doubt that we will see his like again, and the world is a considerably sadder place for his passing.

All Good Things Must...

I don't suppose I ever imagined that working in the plastics warehouse would be my entire career. In all honesty, it was always a panicked measure to avoid being unemployed as soon as I left college. My main problem was, and is, that I've never really known what I want to do. I guess my main priorities were for a 'nice dry job without any heavy lifting', which my current occupation failed on all counts. Nevertheless, staying put was easier than setting myself adrift in the big wide world of commerce, but events were conspiring to move me on to pastures new.

Anyone who knew me in those days would readily tell you that, chief amongst my many failings was a complete inability to be anywhere on time. This can be a problem if you have to clock in to your workplace and lose a quarter of an hour's pay if you're more than three minutes late, which was the arrangement at the warehouse. Given that I always went home for lunch (which was only ten minutes or so down the road), I had the opportunity to be late twice a day, and I took it. The overall effect was that I stood a good chance of owing the company money at the end of the week, rather than drawing any!

Inevitably, this resulted in a number of 'chats" with the Warehouse Manager. It was actually quite rare to see the Warehouse Manager at all. He spent most of his time in a small alcove, off from the main warehouse, where he devoted his days to smoking, drinking tea and keeping the stock records up to date. I suspect he had decided, at an early stage, that man-management was an overrated pastime, particularly when it came to our motley crew, and had wisely decided to delegate that responsibility to our

Team Leader. The fact that he felt compelled to leave his comfort zone and tackle me about my punctuality was a sure sign of the seriousness of the situation.

In addition, my productivity was significantly lower than my colleagues'. Try as I might, I just couldn't pack parcels as fast as they did, I wasn't as strong or adept, although I suppose having no interest whatsoever in the process might have been a contributory factor.

I could see the writing on the wall and I really didn't want to go down the road of 'going down the road' in my first job. I therefore took a few days holiday and set about finding myself another role.

I can't remember if I was sent for interview by the Labour Exchange or whether I applied for jobs advertised in the Burton Daily Mail, but I suspect it was the former. Suitably smartly attired, I attended for interview one morning for a position as a Statistical Clerk at Harold Wesley Ltd., in Victoria Crescent. As luck would have it, my next interview was in the afternoon at BTR Silvertown, which was just around the corner, for a job as a Progress Chaser. I decided to while away the time between the two interviews with a cob and a pint in The Crescent pub, which was a mistake.

The interview at Harold Wesley's had gone reasonably well and so, stoked with confidence and couple of pints of Bass, I approached my next interview with gay abandon. My first problem was that I had no idea what being a Progress Chaser entailed. However, I soon began to find out that you had to be confident with people, and hard-headed enough to take any and all abuse you might engender from those whose progress you were chasing. As I was terminally shy and wouldn't say boo to a goose, my unsuitability became evident to my interviewers and this, coupled with the gales of alcohol which must have been assailing their nostrils with my every answer, pretty much sealed my fate.

I wasn't at all surprised to get a letter of rejection from BTR Silvertown and was, in all honesty, somewhat relieved. However, I was delighted to be invited back for a second interview by Harold Wesley Ltd.

Paper Mates

It's Only A Paper Moon

As I couldn't possibly take any more time off from my job as a Packer, I had to ask if my second interview could be on a Saturday morning, to which they agreed.

Reporting to their offices, which once belonged to the now long-gone Crescent Brewery, I was met by my first interviewer, Mr. Toon. He ushered me in to the upstairs office of Mr. Kimber, the Managing Director. Mr. Kimber was an affable chap who, more or less, chain-smoked throughout our chat. I gathered that he had recently taken over the post of MD from his father and had big plans to change the way that the factory was managed. The position that I had applied for, that of Statistical Clerk, was the first step in that process, this being an entirely new position.

Harold Wesley Ltd's offices, just before demolition.

My first office was the double window on the right hand side of the ground floor

It occurred to me, long after, that I wouldn't have even considered me for the job. Maths was never my strong point and I had been fortunate to crawl out of school with a CSE Grade 2. In addition, my last six months as a Packer in a warehouse hardly augured well for a career in statistics. Nevertheless, the second interview went very well and I was delighted to get a letter early the next week, offering me the job.

The salary wasn't brilliant. In fact, without the overtime I was currently getting at the warehouse, I would probably be worse off, but there was no lifting bales or toting barges and I would finally get to work in an office! I accepted with alacrity, despite my dad's gloomy observation that "no-one wants to work there, you know. It's where people go who can't get a job anywhere else." You know that line about "where never is heard a discouraging word"? Well, it didn't apply at our house, although I think mum was pleased that I was trying to make something of myself.

A couple of weeks' later, having waved a tearful farewell to the plastics warehouse, I stepped off the No. 5 bus in Horninglow Street and presented myself at my new place of work. It felt odd not to be in my usual 'scruff' but instead in a brown sports jacket and nearly matching trousers (I didn't have a work suit to my name). The collar and tie would take a bit of getting used to, having not really featured in my life since I left school.

The first thing on the agenda was a tour of the factory, so that I could appreciate what they did. I have to say it was both fascinating and intimidating. I had never seen anything like it before, and I doubt I ever will again. Much of the factory and equipment looked as if it had come straight from the 19th Century and I'm sure many of the processes had not changed much since that time.

The main products were, as I learned, Crepe Paper, Christmas Decorations (made from the crepe paper), Wrapping Paper and Serviettes. In a very minor way, they also made those flat packs of toilet tissue which you thankfully don't see any more (I think Bronco was the market leader). All in all, an eclectic mix.

I was also shown to my new office. Actually, this wasn't an office at all, it was principally a sort of product showroom and meeting room, but they didn't have anywhere else to put me, so I was to camp in their for the time being, ready to be evicted when the need arose.

Creeping Out For A Crepe

I wish I could take you back to the early 1970s at Wesley's. You see, it was a bit like going into a time machine. The building dated from the 19th century and it often seemed as if much of the equipment and a few of the staff did too!

I'll tell you what, you can follow me around as I pick up last week's production figures from the various departments and I'll show you what I mean.

Coming out of my office, we're crossing the yard and going up those steps on the right. This is the Crepe Paper Dept. Sheila is the supervisor, she's a lovely, cuddly, middle-aged lady who keeps everything running smoothly and knows everything about this place (so she's been a fountain of knowledge to me).

Along the length of the room there are benches placed end-on, so that lengths of crepe paper can be laid along them. At the end of each bench there is a thing like an overgrown rolling pin which is being turned at a furious speed by a belt attached to a continuously moving shaft in the ceiling which runs the length of the room. The idea is that the girls take one end of the length of wrapping paper and apply it to the roller, which whips it into a loose roll which can then be flattened out to produce a fold of crepe paper. That the girls can do this whilst chatting to each other amazes me. The noise is appalling and continuous, but it seems a happy atmosphere.

The bit the girls seem to like most is when they're cutting the lengths of paper in the first place. This involves rolling the paper around a drum of the relevant circumference (6', 8' and so on) then cutting across it and carrying the resultant pile of paper back to their table. The main thing here is the opportunity for a natter and a break from the monotony of rolling crepe folds as the girls wait for their turn to wind their paper onto the drum.

Just around the corner of the room is another source of continuous noise, the sewing section. This is quite skilled work and most of the ladies have been here some time. What happens is that different coloured lengths of crepe paper, about four inches or so in width, are sewn along the centre to cause them to sort of pleat and form a ribbon garland, which was a pretty ubiquitous Christmas decoration when I was young but something you hardly ever see now.

If we go back across the yard, we can see where all this crepe paper comes from. Just through this wooden door are the paper mills which convert ordinary paper into coloured crepe paper. This is a room full of steam and noise and the smell of dye. The foreman hands me a neat sheet of paper with all of the details of last week's production on it. It's a wonder it's as clean and neat as it is, as he is perpetually covered in the various dyes used in the process. I would be hard pressed to explain how they make crepe paper but I know it has to do with the paper being stretched over large drums using steam.

Turning to our right, we pass one of the huge and very complex machines which are turning out thousands of serviettes an hour. The room just beyond is filled with dozens of girls packing these serviettes into polythene outers. There's a smell of melted plastic in the air as the bags are sealed. Doreen, the supervisor, has this department running like a well-oiled machine and her production figures are always immaculate.

If you're wondering if there are any blokes working here at all, well, yes there are, but they tend to be machine operators, or in the engineering and fitting shops, or managers of course, we'll meet them later. We're a long way from anything like equal opportunities, but we've a new Factory Manager starting soon, so who knows, we may edge ourselves into the 20th Century!

<u>*Caught Wrapping*</u>

I absolutely love quirky old industrial buildings that have loads of nooks and crannies (or crooks and nannies, as the old joke goes), with stairways that sometimes lead nowhere and others that take you to places you had no idea even existed.

Harold Wesley Ltd. in its heyday

Old brewery buildings seem particularly prone to this. Whether this is because they grew organically over the years, or whether brewery architects just had a weakness for maze-like interiors, I don't know. Wesley's was exactly like this, which was hardly surprising given that it housed the Crescent Brewery up until the 1920s (a fact which passed me by, at the time, despite the legend 'CRESCENT

BREWERY' being emblazoned across the top of the office building).

Such were the twists and turns of the place that, in my first few months, I frequently got lost, wandering hopelessly on silent, dusty floors stacked with rolls of paper and not a soul in sight.

The part that impressed me most about Wesley's was the Printing Department, largely because it was such a wonderful mixture of ancient and modern technology. At the time, Wesley's printed three types of wrapping paper (mostly Christmas). These were surface print, flexographic and gravure.

Surface print was the type of wrapping paper you probably remember if you grew up in the post-war era. It was crinkly, slightly embossed, quite thin and felt cheap (a bit like me!) I suppose that, at one time, it was the only wrapping paper that was available. The printing machines for this had to be seen to be believed. As the paper passed between the rollers to be printed and embossed, it was then taken up by things like huge coat-hangers which produced folds that must have been about twenty feet high. Each fold was then carried slowly around a large U-shaped track in the ceiling (as if a giant was about to embark on some paper hanging) until the paper was dry and could be wound back on a reel. There was a row of these machines, all generating these huge paper trails winding majestically around the room. It was quite a sight.

Flexographic printing generated a smooth, high quality print, like the wrapping paper we use today and gravure was the very best quality. Wesley's had just taken delivery of a new gravure printer, which was the department's pride and joy. Not new, of course. Wesley's was renowned for being 'careful' with its money and this machine had previously printed newspapers in Fleet Street. It was by this legendary machine that I saw something that I found both hilarious and unbelievable, at the same time.

Mr. P., the Printing Department manager, was a small grey-haired gentleman of enormous energy. He ran everywhere and seemed to be constantly in motion, even when standing still. Arriving at the Department to collect the weekly production figures, I found him supervising the stacking of some printing paper by the gravure printer. Rolls of paper, about 3 feet high, covered the floor as far as the eye could see. Mr P. passed me a slip of paper with the figures on, but I noticed that something had been missed. He said he would go and get it and, to my surprise, bounded onto the first of the reel and raced across the array, toward his office. What he didn't know was that, for whatever reason, there was a roll missing in the middle of the formation. I watched with horror as the rapidly diminishing figure of Mr. P. suddenly vanished altogether with a thud, then, after a few moments, bounced back on top and continued his race to the office. Minutes later, he returned by the same route, carefully avoiding the gap this time, and solemnly handed me the missing figure. Neither he nor I mentioned his fall, and no-one would have been any the wiser, other than a certain dustiness about his jacket and a slight disarray of his hair.

Mr. P's active life style must have suited him as, the last I heard, he was well over 100 and still enjoying a daily walk. For me, however, he will always be a diminutive figure suddenly vanishing amidst a sea of paper.

Automatically, Sunshine!

There's been a lot in the papers recently about the rise of the robots in the workplace and how these might displace jobs in the future. Yet, as I recall, from the predictions on things like 'Tomorrow's World', we should all be sunning ourselves on the beach by now whilst the machines do all the work. It seems to me that most of the things that are supposed to result in fewer people and more leisure time (remember the 'paperless office'?) actually seem to achieve the reverse, but I suppose only time will tell. However, I do think there are some jobs that really don't make the best use of the people employed to do them.

You see, Wesley's was notoriously tight-fisted when it came to capital investment. Most of their machinery must have pre-dated the last unpleasantness in 1939-1945, with just a few exceptions to the rule, such as the second-hand printing press I mentioned . Old machinery tended to come from an era when people were cheap and machines were expensive, so fiddly labour-saving extras were few and far between.

For example, if we walk along the corridor from the Printing Dept., we come to a room where the wrapping paper is converted from rolls into sheets. There are three chaps here who are the mainstay of the department, Frank, Albert (who is in charge) and one other whose name escapes me. All three must be nearing retirement age and seem to have been at Wesley's man and boy. Their role here is to diligently count the sheets coming off the machine and place a cardboard tab in the pile for every 480 sheets (this being the quantity of a ream, in those pre-metric days). I'm sure there was more to it, but that activity seemed to sum up the bulk of their work. I know it must have paid the bills but can you imagine how boring it must have been? There really ought to be a better use of people than that!

Mind you, Frank and Albert's work would have seemed positively enriching compared to what Greta had to put up with, downstairs. From time to time, an ancient piece of machinery, which folded wrapping paper into neat squares, was dusted off and put to use. This machine worked perfectly well, but it had one vital element missing. It had no means of feeding the sheets into the machine, automatically. Greta seemed to be either the only one who knew how the machine worked, or was possibly the only one who was prepared to use it. Her role was to push each sheet into the machine, with her forefinger, time after time. The constant procession of a brightly coloured design making its way across her line of sight, along with the mind-crushing boredom, had a tendency to send her into something of a trance allegedly. I think it would have sent me into a padded room.

Managers have a tendency not to understand that workplaces are as much a social hub as a place of business, and that you mess around with that at your peril. You may recall the Crepe Paper Dept., where the girls wound the crepe onto a drum of a certain diameter, then cut across the swatch to give them a pile of sheets which they folded by means of something akin to a fast spinning wooden rolling pin? Waiting for your turn to wind your particular colour paper was a chance for the girls to have a natter and a break from monotonously folding sheet after sheet. At least, it was until Wesley's employed a Work Study Engineer (I was his assistant, I seem to have specialised in finding unpopular jobs for myself over the years) who redesigned the process so that one girl did all of the winding for the entire department, ensuring the others were not distracted from their task of folding the sheets. I'm sure it was more efficient, but I'll bet it wasn't anywhere near as interesting, and that would be saying something!

A Voice From The Gods

When we think of management these days, we probably have a picture in our minds of young, thrusting types in sharp suits with a mobile phone permanently clamped to their ear. Well, I do anyway. I don't suppose any of us would have had in mind the tier of management that existed at Wesley's. There were four managers, all of whom must have been getting perilously close to retirement age (or, at least, it seemed that way to my teenage eyes).

Firstly, there was Mr. T., who was in charge of the Crepe Paper Dept. He was a large man in all respects, tall but also quite broad, with a permanently worried expression. Mr. T. had been appointed as my mentor in the first few months of my employment, largely because I was relieving him of the task of producing the weekly production statistics. He was always very kind to me and taught me a lot about the company. His size was always a source of concern, and he once had the embarrassing experience of going through one of the ancient wooden floors in the warehousing section of the building. Fortunately, it was just one leg that went through and he wasn't badly hurt, but his pride must have taken a knock.

Mr. D. was in charge of the warehouse and therefore, by extension, the warehouse operatives. This was a gang of around a dozen or so, mostly young, men who were primarily employed to shift huge reels of paper about the place. Mr. D. was a gruff Londoner whose bark was probably just as bad as his bite. He had something of the Sergeant Major about him and I definitely tried not to get on his wrong side, although I'm not entirely sure he had a right side. His approach to man-management would probably have worked well in the 1940s and 1950s but had little chance of success with young men in the 1970s. As a consequence, there was a sort of low-level guerrilla warfare in place in which Mr. D. tried to get things done by shouting and complaining and they largely ignored him and tried to avoid doing anything.

I told you about the hyperactive Mr. P. of the Printing Department and his unfortunate fall whilst running across an array of paper reels. In many ways, he seemed to be the youngest of the four and yet he must have been about the same age. Clearly, hyperactivity has its benefits.

The fourth and final member of the management team was the softly-spoken Mr. C. whose remit would nowadays be called Logistics, but was then known as Despatch. Mr. C. spent most of his working life on the phone, chasing deliveries and arranging pick-ups. This always intrigued me because, as I've already said, he was very softly-spoken and yet he had a habit of holding the phone so that the mouthpiece was as far away from his mouth as possible. With the handset at a 90^0 angle to his face, it was a wonder anyone ever heard anything. Amazingly, Mr. C. and his wife also ran a pub in Anslow, goodness knows where he found the energy, or the time, to do that as well.

Contacting any of these worthies, if they were not by their phone in the office, was a difficult task in the low-tech 1970s. Fortunately, we had a solution. There was a microphone in Reception, and another outside Mr. D's office in the warehouse, which could be used to call any manager over the Public Address System, to the telephone. The normal content of the message was something like *"Calling Mr. T., Mr. T., please ring (whichever extension)"* I usually avoided using this, if at all possible, out of sheer embarrassment, until one occasion, when I had no choice but to make an announcement, and a girl in the Serviette Department made the mistake of saying she liked my voice. Of course, from then on you couldn't keep me off the microphone, convinced as I now was that I was Burton's answer to Terry Wogan!

War in the Warehouse

On reflection, my comment about a "a sort of low-level guerrilla warfare" might have been a bit of an understatement!

As I've mentioned, Mr. D., the Warehouse Manager, belonged to that school of post-war British managers whose 'bark was worse than their bite'. This worked fine in the days of deference but was wearing a bit thin by the early 1970s. The lads (and it was mostly young men) who were employed to shunt huge reels of paper around the ancient building, were not prepared to be constantly bullied and badgered, particularly as they were earning a pittance and their working conditions left a lot to be desired. In those days, Wesley's did not have a trade union or any form of employee representation, which was unusual given that the 1970s recorded the peak of trade union membership. With no official outlet for their grievances, some of the lads turned to mischief to make their point.

The first time I became properly aware of this, other than noticing the constant grumbling coming from both Mr. D. and the warehouse gang, was when I heard scuffling and suppressed giggling coming from Mr. D's office. At the time, I was ensconced in the Works Manager's office (we were a little short of office space) next door to Mr. D's office. I didn't think much about it until Mr. D. returned and uttered a stream of oaths and obscenities. Sticking my head into the lion's den, I discovered that Mr. D's office had been trashed, with papers strewn everywhere and a bottle of ink liberally sprayed over the walls. It was pretty obvious who the culprits were, but nobody could be individually identified because, unsurprisingly, no-one had seen anything. I was quizzed but couldn't shed any light on the investigation.

As it turned out, this was the least serious skirmish in the battle. Unbeknown to Wesley's management, we had our own tame arsonist in the warehouse gang. This would be a problem in any organisation, but when you're a paper conversion factory housed in a building with ancient wooden flooring throughout, it represents a particular menace.

Any fire on the premises occasioned a full station turnout by the fire service and this started to be a regular occurrence. Firstly it was just minor outbreaks, which could easily be contained, but the severity of the incidents increased, until one occasion when much of the warehouse was alight over more than one floor. Flames could clearly be seen licking at the windows of the old brewery building as we stood in the street watching the firemen do their work. The corner of the warehouse that was alight was just a few feet away from the office block. Only the entrance to the main yard separated the two buildings.

Later, when the fire had been brought under control, the fire station chief (who was in a particularly bad humour at having been called out to us yet again) stomped around asking everyone what action they had taken on hearing the fire alarm. He focused his ire on the inhabitants of the office building and, in particular at the office junior and a sort of office junior's assistant employed in the General Office. Two very young girls who were rather immature for their age.

"What did you do when the fire alarm sounded?" The fire station chief barked at them.

"We went and stood in the kitchen." The office junior offered. The fire station chief was aghast. The kitchen was an extension at the back of the office block which was, if anything, nearer the seat of the flames than anywhere else in the building.

"And what did you do in there?" The fire station chief asked, incredulously.

"Well," the office junior simpered, "we held hands"

I thought he would have apoplexy.

We never did find the arsonist. The fires did stop, eventually, which probably meant the culprit either got fed up with it, or more likely, left, but the all-pervading lingering smell of smoke in the place was a lasting reminder of his work.

Let's focus, for a moment, on the accompanying photo as this is a prime example of the 'Christmas Do' at its best (or possibly worst). The year must be 1973 or 1974 and we are at The Newton Park Hotel for Harold Wesley's Christmas Dinner and Dance. This is a surprisingly 'posh' venue for a company that was not known for its generosity when it came to its employees. For the avoidance of doubt (as all good solicitors say) the person on the far left, who looks rather like a Cocker Spaniel sniffing a woolly caterpillar, is me.

Having seen the photo, you may wonder how I managed to inveigle myself onto a table where the ratio of attractive women to men is 2:1? In all honesty, it had nothing to do with my dazzling good looks and everything to do with being a friend of Colin, at the other end of the table.

I'm actually squirming with embarrassment, in the photo, on two counts. Firstly, I have been encouraged to put my arm around the lady sitting next to me, which is fine but we're not actually together in any sense. In fact, she is heavily pregnant (a condition which has been cunningly disguised by judicious arrangement of the tablecloth) so I'm feeling more than a little bit awkward. She is, in fact, the elder sister of Colin's girlfriend, sitting on his right. Secondly, you may note the half-bottle of spirits on the right hand side of the table, near to a voluminous handbag. The size of the handbag is important because this was used to smuggle it in. The girls had all taken this precaution, as they clearly had a good idea of the likely cost of drinks at a hotel in the run-up to Christmas , had ordered an orange juice each at the start of the evening and then proceeded to dilute same with vodka thereafter. As a fully paid up 'goody two shoes' I found this excruciatingly embarrassing and was constantly waiting for the Management's hand to fall on our shoulders and escort us from the building.

You may also notice the three-piece suit I'm wearing. The suit was one of my first investments as a wage-earner and I rather think that this was its first official outing. I had never owned a suit until I went to Burton's Menswear one

Saturday and allowed myself to be talked into this made-to-measure, flared trousered, creation, for a small deposit and regular weekly payments. I was even sold the accompanying shirt and tie on the same easy terms. Unfortunately, it didn't have the most auspicious of beginnings.

Having taken pre-Christmas delivery, I was keen to christen it. It was Saturday night, which was traditionally a night for getting dressed up and going out on the town, but the suit might have been seen as a little OTT, as I was only going down to The Coopers' Arms with my mate, Kevin. For reasons that escape me, Kevin was getting ready at our house and was having a shave using our kitchen sink (bathrooms being an unimaginable luxury for us at that point). I had already changed into the ensemble you see in the photo and was standing chatting to Kev, with me leaning against the draining board. What I didn't realise was that Kev had the curious habit of lighting a cigarette and leaving it burning, whilst shaving, propped up in the corner of the draining board with the lit end uppermost. The first I knew about this was when my arm became uncomfortably hot and I realised that smoke was billowing from my sleeve. Kev's cigarette had burned a neat semi-circle into the sleeve of my brand new suit and shirt! To say that I was a bit miffed would be understating it somewhat. That we're still friends some 40+ years on, says something about the healing spirit of Christmas.

Three Days A Week!

There has been a lot of talk recently about Britain returning to the 1970s. I don't think it's very likely, I would never get the flares to fit me now for one thing!

The 1970s were a peculiar decade in many ways and, of course, there aren't as many of us about today who remember them and lived through them. At one time, the mention of 'the three day week' would have had everyone nodding glumly and bringing up their own particular stories of privations endured. Now it's more likely to have people scratching their heads and wondering if you've finally lost it and are actually talking about the war.

I told you about the trashing of the Warehouse Manager's office, which was next to the Works Manager's office in which I was temporarily installed (much to the chagrin of the Works Manager, but there was a shortage of office space). What I didn't mention was that one reason for not noticing who was involved was that the whole office section was, at that time, enclosed in a stygian gloom caused by the myriad effects of the short winter days, the lack of outside light from the few windows and, more importantly, the complete lack of any artificial light because of the three day week.

For those who don't remember this period, or are desperately trying to forget it, the 'three day week'

47

happened in the winter of 1973-1974. To be honest, the details had escaped me so I've had to break the habits of a lifetime and actually do some research! We were at the end (although we didn't know it at the time) of the Heath government of 1970 – 1974. The miners had announced an overtime ban in support of a pay claim and the government of the time tried to eke out the country's fuel reserves by restricting the use of coal and power. "Commercial consumption of electricity would be limited to three consecutive days each week…Television shut at 10:30 p.m. each night, and most pubs were closed" (https://en.wikipedia.org/wiki/Three-Day_Week)

Can you imagine trying to impose something like that now? The outcome was that for two days each week the factory was plunged into darkness, illuminated by the occasional battery driven lamp. Work was organised to take place in the few hours of daylight and largely consisted of whatever jobs could be done by hand and which didn't involve machines. As I was still producing statistics by dint of laborious manual addition and long-division, the lack of technology wasn't a problem but the lack of light and the lack of heating, was. On top of this, rolling power cuts at home meant that you could get home only to find yourself plunged into darkness once more.

In January, 1974, the miners went on strike and the whole situation deteriorated further. You have to remember that strikes then were all or nothing affairs. Nowadays we're used to strikes being one-day annoyances but then they were wars of attrition, in which both sides waited to see who would blink first. In this case, it was the government, which went to the country in February, 1974 with the question "Who governs Britain?" Of course, if you ask a silly question…the electorate clearly decided it whoever it was, it wasn't the Heath government.

Over the years, Ted Heath has come in for a lot of criticism but, apart from plunging me into darkness and trying to freeze me to death, I did have cause to remember him fondly. You see, Wesley's were renowned as poor payers and my salary was pitiful in comparison to my mates. However, in November, 1973 good old Ted brought in a concept called Threshold Payments. The idea here was to protect the lowest paid from the rampaging inflation of the time. This basically meant that every time that inflation went up by one per cent above 7%, wages could, and did, rise in tandem. Over a very short period, my wages basically doubled, albeit from a very low starting point, and, as the only inflation that affected me was the price of a pint, I had never had it so good (to borrow another P.M.'s phrase).

Cheers, Ted!

The Man in the Nearly Suit

In these enlightened times, when casual dress is often the recommended work attire and offices are more likely to have a table tennis than a boardroom table, it's difficult to remember just how hierarchical the workplace used to be.

You see, there were people in suits, usually male, who were the management and others in overalls who were the workers. Then there was me. I'm pretty sure that the people on the 'shop floor' at Wesley's didn't really know what to make of me. Was I part of the distrusted 'management', or was I one of the workers?

To be fair, I was never too sure myself, largely because I was actually unique. I was the only male clerical worker in the company. I didn't wear a suit, because I only had my one 'made to measure' three-piece indulgence from my first job, which was only suitable for high days and holidays and would have looked distinctly OTT in a work context. However, I did feel as if I *ought* to wear a suit, so I got as close as I could with a brown sports jacket and some brown trousers which were nearly, but not quite, the same colour.

Philip's 'Nearly Suit'

The confusion about my managerial status was also compounded by the fact that, when all of the Departmental Managers were called to the General Office for morning and afternoon tea, so was I. However, the really confusing feature, and the only occasion when I came even close to being part of 'the management', was when it came to stocktaking.

Stocktaking took place twice a year, usually on a Saturday when the factory wasn't working. The system was that the Head of Department for each area counted the various piles of stock in his (and it was always 'his') department. He then completed a three-part form which showed what the stock was and where it was but only put the quantity on the top sheet, leaving the other two parts with the stock. Then a second person would come along, count the stock again and put their total on the second part of the form. Parts one and two would be sent up to the Managing Director's office for him to compare the totals and the third part would remain with the stock to show it had been counted. Fascinating, eh? I was never entrusted with the initial count, I was the follow-on.

The best part of this arrangement, however, was that you were assigned a gopher! You see, it was never expected that members of management would be required to clamber over stacks of paper reels and suchlike. That would never do. Instead, each stock-taker had with him one or two lads from the warehouse gang. It was their job to clamber over the stacks, count and report back.

The beauty of this was that you stood a better chance of tracking down exactly where stuff had been stacked (especially if you had a friendly 'gopher') because they had, in all probability, been part of the gang who put it there in the first place. The other benefit was that the warehouse lads knew if the stock had been there since God was a lad, and therefore the total hadn't changed in decades.

I couldn't help feeling more than a little awkward about this arrangement. It made perfect sense for some of the more venerable managers we had in the company, who really couldn't be expected to indulge in the mountaineering antics required in some parts of the warehouse, but I was about the same age as most of the lads in the warehouse, and considerably younger than some. I therefore felt rather guilty as they climbed up the stacks, with commendable agility, whilst I stood a discreet distance away from all the dust and cobwebs and inscribed the figure they came up with on the form. It was a dirty job, but somebody had to do it!

Late and Seen

Actually, it's not quite true that nobody was really sure whether I was a manager or not when I worked at Harold Wesley Ltd. The senior management and I were in no doubt as to where I fitted in the pecking order.

I think my mum had aspirations though. That became clear when I received, unexpectedly one birthday, a very nice quality small suitcase with incorporated document case. I think she rather thought this was what the aspiring young executive should have. However, a document case rather implies that you have work to bring home and I barely had enough to do in my normal hours of work, without traipsing any home with me. I did try to act the part for a while by transporting my lunchtime sandwiches in the suitcase, but it just made it look as if I was constantly leaving home, so I abandoned that idea.

In truth, any hopes of advancement I might have had would have been kippered by my inability to arrive at work on time. You may recall that I had the same problem at the Plastics Warehouse? Well, this was exacerbated by Wesley's being the first job where it wasn't practicable to walk or cycle to work; I had to catch the bus.

Catching the bus should not have been a problem, and wouldn't have been to most people. The best to catch was the No. 5 at the bus stop diagonally opposite from All Saints' Church on Branston Road. This left at about 8.10 and would get me comfortably to Dean and Smedley's on Horninglow Road, around the corner from Wesley's, just before 8.30 (which is when I was due to start work). However, for every time when I caught this bus, there were at least a couple of times when I didn't.

I should have been a world-class athlete as a consequence of running to try and catch the bus. Never good at getting out of bed in the morning (I'm still not) I would leave my departure from our house in South Broadway St. until the very last moment. A fast-ish walk down South Broadway St, whilst lighting a cigarette, usually turned to a steady lope along All Saints' Road which then became a flat-out sprint as I saw the bus go past the church at the top of the road. Sometimes there would be other passengers waiting at the bus stop and I would have sufficient time to get to the bus before it pulled away. On other occasions, dependent on the degree of sadistic pleasure on the part of the driver, it would either wait for me to make it to the bus stop and fall aboard gasping for breath or, more frequently, pull away just as I was within a few yards of victory, leaving me doubled up with exhaustion and frustration.

If I missed the No. 5, I was left with the prospect of catching either a No. 12 or a No. 6. Neither of these would get me to work on time, or anything like it and would also entail getting off in Waterloo Street to then walk, or more likely run, up Victoria Crescent.

I would then have to try and insinuate myself into the factory in a way that didn't call attention to my late arrival. The best option was to make my way up the loading dock, hoping not to bump into anyone, and then, with a piece of paper gripped in my hand, walk determinedly toward my office as if I had just been somewhere to collect some vital statistics.

I was now sharing an office with Gwen and, for this ruse to work, I had to hope she wouldn't call attention to my late arrival. In her memoir *'Wednesday's Child'* she writes, *"I'm sure Philip didn't take kindly to me joining him as he liked being on his own – I suspect he thought I might grass him up when he sneaked in through the back door – late most days"*. Fortunately, she didn't!

Did I meet my mum's aspirations and get to wear a proper suit at last, or did my persistent lateness consign me to a life down at the dole office?

You can find out by following the rest of the story as it appears, each month, in the Derby Telegraph or in my blog 'The Slightly Odd World of Phil Whiteland', or wait for the next collection of stories.

PLAY

Back to the Balearics

You may recall (well, I hope you do, that is what the bulk of this book is all about after all) that I spent a good proportion of my early days at Harold Wesley Ltd., in Victoria Crescent, Burton, in the not-so-splendid isolation of my 'office', which was really a meeting room/product showroom with a desk tucked in under the windows for my use.

I think it says something about my career choice, back in 1972, that the highlight of my week was calculating lengthy long-division sums by hand. As I said, previously, spending at least two days per week with nothing to do, whilst trapped in an office on your own, with no excuse to go out of it, nor any need for anyone to come and see you, is enough to drive anyone to the edges of their sanity, and I probably didn't have as far to go as most.

Fortunately, there was one small light on the horizon. Something to look forward to even when I was sure I was losing the plot. For this, we need to take a quick trip back to my former job at the DIY Plastics warehouse.

Regular readers, and there must be at least one of you, may remember the week's holiday I spent in Arenal, Majorca with my mate Kev during the summer holidays when we were both at Burton Technical College (see 'Forty Years On' in <u>Crutches for Ducks</u>)? In conversation with the gang at the warehouse, I waxed lyrical about this holiday, the sun, sea and sangria, and how ridiculously cheap it all was. One of the gang, who had been a good friend to me as I was learning the job and who, for the sake of protecting the innocent, I'll call Den, was particularly interested.

The end result was that Kev, Den and I decided that it would be fun to repeat the experience. The difference this time was that, because we had more funds to splash about (previously it had been just what we could earn in the few weeks of holiday) we could afford to have ten days instead of just a week, and we elected to go to a more exclusive (well, it was in 1972) part of Majorca. Accordingly, we booked ourselves in to the Pollensa Park Hotel in Puerto de Pollensa. This was largely because it looked as if it was right on to the beach from the picture in the brochure (it wasn't) and because it was within our budget.

Three is a difficult number for any group. The potential for two to align themselves against the other one, is always quite high. Our group was inevitably going to be a tricky one because we had very little in common. I only knew Den as a work colleague, and I now no longer worked there, whereas I had known Kev for a couple of years by now and quite a bit of water (and beer) had flown under the bridge. Kev, of course, only knew Den through me and so they had no common ground at all. To try to overcome this, we met up on a relatively regular basis in the months preceding our holiday. Thankfully, we all liked a drink and a game of darts, which was a good starting point, and we seemed to get on. As it turned out, the main irritant in the group, once we were on holiday, was me!

My memories of this holiday are a bit fragmented, for reasons that will become obvious later. I'm not even certain which airport we flew from. At that time, I was panic-stricken by the thought of flying and took my then usual precaution of trying to anaesthetise myself to the whole experience by consuming quite a large quantity of alcohol before the flight. It must have worked, because I don't remember anything about it.

What I do recall is that we nearly missed our transfer bus from Palma airport because we were held up at Customs (I think there was some sort of strike in progress). This could have been potentially very serious as we had no concept of just how far away our hotel was from the airport (56 kms apparently). Finally, jammed on to a coach full of people, mostly of our own age, we set off, as night fell, for the long trip across the island of Majorca.

In the Drink!

The accompanying picture should give you a fair idea of the theme of this section. I'm willing to bet that anyone who had a holiday in Spain in the 1970s has one of these buried, and thankfully forgotten, somewhere amongst their holiday snaps. Before you ask, it is not a photograph of someone trying to put out a fire in a horse-hair mattress, but we'll come to the explanation later.

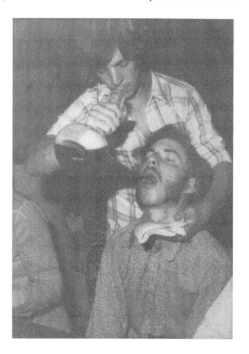

We arrived at our hotel late in the evening and discovered, to our chagrin, that we had a room with one double bed and one single camp-type bed.   Kev was first through the door and was quick to claim the camp bed as his own, which left Den and me with the double.   Common sense should have told us to ring Reception and ask for the bed to be converted to twin singles, but we were young and unsophisticated and, as this was only the second time I had been in a hotel in my life, we just decided we would have to make the best of it.

Kev decreed that he had had enough for one day and decided to turn in for the night, but Den and I were excited about arriving in Majorca and set off for the pub across the road, El Leon Dorado.   Whether this was a good idea, or not, can be judged by the fact that we burst in on Kev an hour or so later, in search of more money for alcohol and declaring that the beer was "just like Pedigree" (our usual tipple at home) It wasn't!

I have always said that the English are really only happy when they are confined by rules and regulations, particularly when it comes to the partaking of alcohol and, by the English, I really mean me. After years of sneaking into pubs whilst under the legal age (I know, I know, I should be ashamed of myself) and dutifully heading for home each evening at 10.30 when the pubs shut, I had rather decided to take full advantage of the more liberal, continental approach to the consumption of alcohol on this holiday, starting from Day 1.   In fact, the first night pretty much set the tone of the rest of the holiday for me.

Den was a keen cyclist, so he wasted no time in hiring a bike and setting off each day to discover more of the island. Kev joined him on a few occasions. I made one trip out to the nearest village with them and decided it was too much like hard work.

Kev and Den were also keen to get a decent tan and, therefore, headed down the lane to the nearby beach quite frequently. I, on the other hand, usually didn't surface until midday and then only to drag myself across the road to El Leon Dorado. Any tan I got was purely accidental, usually as a result of the sun having moved so that the parasol at my bar table was no longer protecting me.

On one occasion, I did get up enough enthusiasm to stagger down to the beach and join them. I dimly recall deciding to have a dip in the Med. and set about demonstrating an enthusiastic front crawl (to the dismay of all in the vicinity) which later turned out to have been in roughly six inches of water, this went some way to explain the extensive cuts to my arms and legs when I tottered back up the beach.

All in all, I was single-handedly confirming the worst perceptions of the British teenager abroad, way before this became fashionable! And the holiday was yet young, we still had two drinking highlights to go, a night at a medieval banquet (hence the photo) and a night out clubbing.

Three highlights (or possibly, lowlights) of that holiday spring to mind.

The first was the Medieval Banquet. This was a pretty ubiquitous feature of Spanish holidays at that time, which involved being carted out to some mountainous retreat where you were treated to chicken in a basket, plied with unlimited amounts of wine on the table, had a waiter pouring more of the same down your throat (cue raucous laughter if you messed this up and finished with it pouring all over you) and finally consumed some dubious spirit to round the night off. Partially fed and enormously drunk, you then staggered out to watch a jousting match with various locals dressed in allegedly medieval costume.

The one we attended was made all the more dramatic by a thunderstorm playing out in the surrounding mountains, ultimately leading to a power-cut (not unusual in Spain at that time, there were power cuts most days) and the whole place being plunged into darkness. The jousting was also more dramatic than intended, as one of the players was knocked off his horse with considerable ferocity and, presumably, hurt himself as he was still on the floor surrounded by a crowd when we had all ambled off to the bar.

The second lowlight was when we discovered a ten pin bowling alley a few streets away from our hotel. I've always enjoyed ten pin bowling, largely because it's the only 'sport' for which I've ever shown any aptitude, so I was particularly pleased about this. The first unusual element was that the whole thing was outdoors, set in a garden of sorts. From the front, it appeared to be a standard bowling alley, with multiple lanes and all of the usual paraphernalia. It was only when we began to bowl that the awful truth emerged. Although it was a regular bowling alley in all other senses, the aspect that was different was that it had no mechanism behind it at all. The whole thing was entirely operated by very young children! Pins were reset and balls returned by kids no more than 5 or 6, who then tucked themselves in behind the pins (where the mechanism should have been) whilst the balls were hurtling down. That this was clearly an unsafe pastime was evident from the number who were sporting plaster casts. Such were the joys of Franco's Spain.

The third and final lowlight was when the three of us decided to go for a night on the town. Dressed to the nines, we made a start at 'El Leon Dorado', our local pub across the road. The idea was that we would then head off to the nightclubs. We ordered a pint and then a round of shorts. I decided to show off by demonstrating how to swallow a whole shot of brandy in one smooth movement. The barman, obviously aware that this was an idiot worth cultivating, kept refilling my glass and I kept 'Bogarting' them down. I even fell for being served a shot of Tabasco (of which I'd never heard) with which I did the same, and then had to pretend that my throat wasn't on fire and my eyes watering fit to burst. All of these brandies had a predictable effect and I dread to think what the Hotel Receptionist thought when, forty five minutes after us leaving, all dressed up for a night out, Kev and Den returned dragging a near-comatose me to be returned to the room.

Apparently, they had a brilliant night out in the nightclubs, whereas all I remember was wakening some time toward noon the following day, still fully dressed and with a mouth like something small, furry and foul-smelling, had hibernated there. Certainly not my finest hour.

At The End Of The Day

Ten days is a weird duration for a holiday, it's neither one thing, nor the other! Before this return to Majorca in the early 1970s, I don't think I had been on a holiday that lasted more than a week, and I've avoided ten days ever since, for reasons which will become obvious.

I suppose that the end of our holiday must have been in our minds because we had begun to think about what we might take back with us. In my case, I had bought a pair of Clackers for my sister. Do you remember Clackers? They were a one summer craze back in the 1970s and were very much in evidence on this holiday. Clackers were two ceramic coloured balls on a piece of rope. You held them by the centre of the rope and the idea was to cause the two spheres to bounce against each other repeatedly, with such force that kinetic energy eventually caused them to fly upward and clash again at the top of the stroke and so on. Sounds fun, eh?

They made a horrific noise. You could hear them all over the resort. The problem was, if you messed up the rhythm, you stood a good chance of striking your wrist a painful blow with one or both balls, which resulted in a good many broken wrists and probably explains the short-lived nature of the craze. On the whole, it was probably an ill-advised present, but it seemed a good idea at the time.

Another clue to the duration of our holiday should have been when our next door neighbours went home. We had been somewhat wary of these lads in the next room. They seemed to keep pretty irregular hours and when they did appear on their balcony, they invariably bellowed "Oh, Samantha! Let me kiss your…" well, we won't go into what they wanted to kiss but this phrase echoed around the holiday complex countless times.

On their last day, we happened to be on our balcony and got chatting. Apparently they had met the hapless Samantha and her mother on their first day, had discovered that they were staying in a hotel opposite ours, and embarked on their campaign thereafter. I should imagine it was a holiday to forget for Samantha's mother.

Our last day was like any other. In fact, too much like any other. We were sitting outside a little bar near our hotel. Kev and Den were sipping cokes, I was on my first Bacardi and Coke of the day (it had been that sort of holiday). We were musing about how long we had been away and started to work it out, when panic set in. Today was our last day and we should have checked out of our room by 10.00! It was now well past that hour. We ran back to the hotel, only to find a clutch of very annoyed Spanish cleaners gathered outside our room. After a good deal of begging and pleading, we were allowed 20 minutes to pack and clear out.

Our flight home was not until late that night, so we stored our luggage and whiled away the day. Kev and Den sunbathed, I propped up a table at El Leon Dorado.

Before our coach came to take us back to Palma, Kev and Den decided they would like to shower and change and somehow managed to persuade a couple of lads from the BBC, who were just commencing their holiday at the hotel, to let them have the use of their room whilst they relaxed in the bar. Being a scruffy urchin, I declined but was left as a sort of surety with these blokes. As time ticked by and Kev and Den failed to appear, my persistent bleats of "I'm sure they'll be here soon" came to seem increasingly desperate and they began to get more than somewhat anxious and angry. Eventually I had to go up and tell Kev and Den, who were just taking their time with their ablutions and sorting out what they were going to wear for the flight home, that we stood a good chance of the police turning up if they didn't come down soon.

So our holiday ended, and I headed back to my solitary office at Harold Wesley Ltd. Back to the long division and splendid isolation but, as you've already seen in the 'Paper Mates' section, things did improve over time.

Given my shame-faced confessions in the previous story, the following seemed appropriate. For a short while, the Derby Telegraph let me loose on their Editorial Column once in a blue moon, this is one of those articles:

Oliver's Army

Many people regard Oliver Cromwell's brief Puritan reign in the 17th Century as just a blip in English history, but I'm convinced that he was tapping in to something deep in our national psyche, which the Cavaliers never successfully eradicated.

If you want proof of this, you need only look at the newspapers and magazines circulating in January. Throughout December, all of these have full colour photographs of lavishly rich food and drink as suggestions for your consumption over Christmas (which now seems to start at some point in August). In January, they're sporting pictures of a lettuce leaf and a couple of radishes alongside earnest advice on how to count the calories and remove that post-Christmas bulge. At the same time, there are a plethora of adverts pushing various aids to quit smoking, along with charities urging people to consider, ironically given the usual levels of flooding, a 'dry' January. In addition, the government are reviewing the official alcohol guidance, and you know that will only be going in one direction.

I think the media know full well that we're never happier than when we're beating ourselves up for enjoying ourselves and so, having urged us on with word and deed in December, they're only too keen to scourge us now that the party's over.

We seem to need to have rules and regulations to keep our wilder side in check. Remove them and we tend to get a bit carried away. For example, the liberalisation of the licensing laws, which it was fondly hoped might generate a Continental café-style culture, has allegedly led to binge-drinking amongst the younger generations and just shifted the night's entertainment back by an hour or so for everyone else.

It also means that we no longer have anything to push against. If closing time is a moveable feast, you can't justify 'having a quick one before they close' as you could be there all night. I've mentioned before about one chap I knew whose wife wouldn't let him go to the pub before 10.25 (in the days when they closed at 10.30) in an effort to curb his drinking. All that happened, of course, was that he ordered four pints on entering and proceeded to consume these with vigour before the end of drinking-up time, by which point he was barely capable of coherent speech. Nowadays, in the absence of a closing time, he would probably vanish through the door of the Public Bar and never be seen again.

If you need proof of our inherent need for rules and regulations, just look at the smoking ban in public places. I felt sure that this would be really difficult, if not impossible, to enforce, particularly in the wilder bars and clubs but no. One day we had pubs where it was difficult to see from one end to the other, the next a complete absence of smoke. Admittedly, this was a mixed blessing in those establishments where the smell of cigarette smoke was hiding a multitude of sins emanating from the carpet...and elsewhere. Nevertheless, a more or less unenforceable rule was adopted, without question, in the blink of an eye. Social pressure is clearly more effective, in some circumstances, that any number of 'bobbies on the beat'.

I think that even those on the losing end of this legislation actually quite enjoy the restrictions. Those people standing outside in the rain, dragging lustily on their cigarettes as their extremities turn blue with cold and dodgy circulation, are enjoying themselves hugely. They are both pandering to their addiction *and being penalised for it at one and the same time*. It doesn't get much better than that.

What would be nice would be if the 'nanny' element of the 'nanny state' could give up nagging and just let us sort things out for ourselves. I'm pretty sure most of us know that an excess of anything is not good for us over the long term, and that probably includes lettuce leaves and radishes, but if we're hemmed in by overly-onerous guidelines and restrictions, we'll just rebel (like my bloke drinking four pints in 25 minutes). We may be puritan at heart, but can't we be a little cavalier once in a while?

Sometimes, something comes out of the blue and simply knocks your socks off. This is one of those occasions:

Barging in to the Cinema

I do love the internet! Having so much information at our finger tips is astounding. Sometimes it seems that everything you can think of is there, if you know where to look. For example…

Out of the blue, I received a message from an old school friend, who now lives in Australia (which, again, is pretty amazing. Years ago, if you had emigrated to the antipodes, you might as well have died for all communication intents and purposes, now you can have a real-time chat by text or face-to-face via Skype!) Some of you may have heard of Kevin Spiers, a very talented professional musician, well known on the Burton music scene? Well, Kevin retains an interest in Burton and its heritage and occasionally finds something squirreled away on the internet. This message was about just such a find and I couldn't have been more amazed.

Regular readers may recall a story from my days at Uxbridge Junior School, around 1964, when our class was taken on a canal trip. This was pretty exciting in itself, but it was made more so by the presence of a film crew from the 'Look at Life' team. Do you remember 'Look at Life'? It was a sort of ten minute documentary review of life in

Britain which helped to fill the gap between the B movie and the main feature.

The film crew remained with us all day and shot quite a bit of film of what was a glorious and very interesting event. Like most of my contemporaries, my previous experience of canals would have been walks along the towpath and futile attempts at fishing, resulting in the watery demise of a few maggots. On this day, we experienced the joys of canal travel and marvelled at the mechanics of ascending a huge flight of locks.

Some months later, further excitement followed when the whole school was invited to an exclusive showing of the relevant 'Look at Life' episode at the Odeon in Guild Street, which was opened especially for us. I guess we all expected that our canal trip would dominate the episode, given how long they had spent filming us. Of course, in reality, nothing could have been further from the truth. I'm not even sure if I actually saw myself on the big screen, I may well have been retrieving a sweet from the floor at the time. It was definitely a case of "if you blink, you'll miss it". I think we were all rather underwhelmed, but it was still something to tell our grandchildren.

I never expected to see this footage again (always assuming that I'd seen it the first time) but Kevin's message revealed that he had found it! There, once again, we can see Mrs. Strong, our teacher, leading a class out onto our school playground to follow the contours of a chalked map of the Midlands, proudly showing the mighty power stations along the banks of the Trent. Kevin makes the point that it must have been a Monday, as you can see washing lines full of sheets in the gardens of Oak Street, which backed on to our playground.

At the bottom of the picture you can see, on the left, David Topliss (in zip up cardigan) me (partially obscured) and, to the right, Alan Lewsley

Then we cut to the canal trip and there, if you look really closely, you can see, at the front of the picture, me sitting between my two friends David Topliss (by the window, looking disgruntled) and Alan Lewsley (looking bemused) Directly behind Alan is Mr. Adams, our headmaster (which may explain the bemusement) resplendent in overcoat, jacket and waistcoat. Then the film moves on to another class (not us) timing objects floating down a river.

I can't begin to describe the sheer pleasure of finally being able to see this well remembered event again after all of these years. Mrs. Strong and Mr. Adams of course seemed as old as Methuselah to us at the time, but I can see that they were considerably younger than I am now.

Were you at Uxbridge Juniors in 1964? Perhaps you're in the film? You can find out by going to You Tube and find BBC Britain on Film, Series 2 Episode 2 Children - Look at Life FULL.

Sweet Truth

Firstly, can I make it clear that I am not now, and have never been, a chocoholic. I know that some of my friends, with whom I have shared a meal, might look at this statement with some surprise, knowing as they do that if there's a chocolate-flavoured option on the Dessert Menu, that's where you'll find me. I dare say that my wife might raise a knowing eyebrow (wives are good at that, from my experience) and point to the latest pack of plain chocolate digestives secreted in the supermarket trolley. I would plead guilty to all of the above, but I would still contend that I'm not a chocoholic, simply because I don't have cupboards crammed with the stuff, and rarely buy a chocolate bar. The few occasions when I do have a bar of chocolate, or something of that ilk, in my possession are usually post-birthday or Christmas, when I've been given them. Even then, I'm afraid that I am one of those annoying people who can eat a few squares and then return the bar to the cupboard *and forget all about it*. This drives my wife nuts! She can't even stand having chocolate in the house as she says it 'calls to her'.

What, you might ask, is the point of all of this? Well, I was reflecting on the sweet-buying habits of my childhood the other day, largely as a result of my grandson trying to decide which particular variety of Haribo sweets he liked. It struck me that many of the Haribo varieties are direct descendants from the range of stuff that used to grace most corner-shop windows.

I used to have mixed feelings about sweet buying. I think this was largely because my best friend, Elaine, in my pre-school years and just after, was part of that rare band of children who were forbidden sweets and had no desire to partake of them. Elaine's parents were somewhat ahead of their time, in the late 1950s/early 1960s, in that they actively encouraged the consumption of fresh fruit, carrots and such as an alternative to sweets. When Elaine first told me (I think I was working on getting my free Beech Nut chewing gum from the machine outside Greening's shop at the time) I was quite shocked. I didn't know such people existed. As a consequence of Elaine's strictly held views about sweets, I always felt like some sort of degenerate when I crept into Greening's, armed with my sixpence pocket money, for my fix of Mars Bar or Milky Way, even if she wasn't there. Nevertheless, I'm sure that Elaine (who must now be in her early 60s) has a set of teeth that make dentists weep, whereas mine used to have them booking their holidays in the Caribbean.

Regular readers may recall that Elaine was the person who introduced me to the dubious delights of dog biscuits as an alternative snack. You can, of course, approach the chewing of dog biscuits with a devil-may-care attitude if your teeth have never had to contend with anything more sugar-laden than an apple.

The problem that I always faced as a child was the internal battle between my desire to get the most sweets for my rather limited funds and my desire for those sweets to be chocolate in nature. I was to learn that you can't have it both ways, which is a valuable lesson in life. You could have wholesale quantities of such things as Black Jacks and Fruit Salad chews for a few pence and I often did, but they were a million miles away from the real thing, which was chocolate, in case your mind had drifted off toward cola bottles. You could have those awful Flying Saucers if you were so inclined or red liquorice shoelaces in abundance. I drew the line at both of those. You could even have a sherbet fountain, complete with liquorice dibber, if the fancy took you, but it wouldn't be chocolate.

Liquorice, in all its forms, made up a lot of the sweet offering within pocket-money range in those days and this was invariably approved of by parents and grandparents alike (except Elaine's). Why? Well, we British are renowned for our obsession with bowel movement, or the lack, thereof. The French, I am reliably informed, have a similar fixation with their livers, whereas the Germans fret about their blood pressure and heart function. Liquorice is, of course, a mild laxative, so anything that promoted bowel regularity had to be a good thing, particularly if the child was blissfully unaware of this subterfuge. Most conventional medicines, of that time, also had an additional laxative function as a matter of course, including cough medicines, presumably on the basis that you would think twice about coughing if your mind was focused on the goings-on at the other end of your anatomy.

Somebody the other day on Facebook was waxing lyrical about Liquorice Wood as a sweet option, which was definitely the laxative form of liquorice stripped bare of all pretence, still it takes all sorts (I'm truly sorry for that).

It will not surprise you to learn that I really couldn't see the point of liquorice. It was ok, if all else failed, but it left a lot to be desired.

Then there were the sweets which were essentially variations on a theme of nougat. Sweet Cigarettes, for example. You could, just about, convince yourself that you looked 'cool' as you shook one of these from the pack and placed it, dangling, in your mouth, like a 1930s gangster, but you could not get away from the fact that they tasted cheap and dreadful and you were fooling nobody. You could also get those pink shrimp type things, which tasted of nothing but sugar. Finally, there were Lucky Bags, the essence of which was that the only people who experienced any good fortune with these were all those in the chain of commerce that sold them to you. They usually consisted of some pointless toy, which broke as soon as you looked at it, along with a few sweets that couldn't be shifted in any other way, typically including a nondescript toffee and a few anonymous chews.

Speaking of toffee, when I said that Elaine was not allowed sweets in any shape or form that was not strictly true. Her grandparents occasionally threw caution to the winds and invested in a slab of Blue Bird Toffee. Do you remember those? They used to come with their own little metal hammer so that you could reduce the slab to bite-sized chunks. I think that a chunk of toffee was a Sunday afternoon treat for Elaine, which I found somewhat underwhelming but if your experience of an illicit luxury up to that point was a dog biscuit, then I guess it had a lot to recommend it.

A Cultural Difference

I found myself in the cultural quarter of Stoke-on-Trent a few weeks ago. This may surprise you in, at least, two ways. Firstly, that I was in a cultural quarter at all, and secondly, that Stoke *has* a cultural quarter.

I was here for the theatre. A dramatisation of 'Room on the Broom' if you must know. Not that I was going to enjoy this thespian endeavour, my role for the day was to chauffeur my grandson and wife to join the rest of his playgroup for their end of term treat. Therefore, whilst they settled themselves into the Regent Theatre, I was left to potter around the pavements in the determined drizzle of a weekday morning.

I may have missed something, but the only cultural aspects of the 'cultural quarter' that I could discern were the theatre and BBC Radio Stoke, but I suppose you've got to start somewhere. I may not be viewing the 'cultural quarter' with entirely unbiased eyes, as I'm a little bitter about BBC Radio Stoke. Many years ago, when I was a presenter for our local Hospital Radio station, I sent a demo tape to Radio Stoke in the hope that they might take pity on me and let me loose on their public. I heard nothing from them, so I wrote to the Station Manager complaining bitterly about being ignored by the local radio station. This seemed to have the desired effect, as I was invited to come in to the station for a chat. They kindly gave me a tour of the station and an explanation of the station's output. The highlight of all of this was when one of their celebrity presenters suddenly dived out of his studio, mid-programme, to come and shake my hand. I was hugely impressed at this welcome from a brother broadcaster, until it turned out that he had mistaken me for the local Euro-MP and his interest in me waned spectacularly when he found out who I was. At the end of the tour, a callow youth was dragged in to meet me and he explained to the Station Manager that he had reviewed my demo tape and had found me to be nothing special, whereupon my visit ended and I was returned to the pavements of Stoke, somewhat deflated.

I'm not actually sure that Stoke's cultural quarter is, in fact, in Stoke. Those of you who know Stoke, or who are fans of the work of Arnold Bennett, will know that Stoke consists of six towns, Hanley, Burslem, Tunstall, Longton and Fenton in addition to Stoke itself. This makes it a nightmare if you're looking for the city centre, as there are six of them. I rather suspect that the cultural quarter is in Hanley, but I'm sure you'll tell me if I'm wrong.

Anyway, sitting in a car park didn't seem to be a very entertaining occupation for an hour or more, so I set out to discover the cultural quarter. Having exhausted its offerings in about ten minutes flat, I fell back on the traditional English solution, and went for a cup of tea. Parked in a cafe, poring over the internet on my mobile phone to give the impression of my having some purpose, I was able to indulge in a little people-watching. The opportunities for this were quite limited, as the only other people in the cafe were three men sitting at the table by the window. It was evident, from their conversation, that a job interview was in progress.

I'm always fascinated by job interviews because they're almost invariably awful. Most of my career has been spent in HR in one form or another, so I have some inkling of the theory and practice of selection interviews, which is more than can be said for most managers. Did you know, for example, that the predictive validity (how likely it is that you can predict success in the job) of most unstructured selection interviews (those that are, by and large, a chat) is about the same as tossing a coin? On that basis, you can guess the likely success of those managers who "can tell what they're like as soon as they walk through the door" - and there are a lot of them still about!

This interview was being conducted by a grey-haired bloke in his shirt sleeves, with his back to me, who seemed to be leading things, along with a slightly younger, balding bloke with glasses and the expression of one who has never seen a spreadsheet he didn't like. The candidate was a young man, apparently a school-leaver, who appeared to be applying for an apprenticeship in website development. By and large, the interview seemed to be reasonably effective, and the young chap gave a good account of himself. However, my respect for him increased immeasurably when the lead bloke asked him:

"How would you make sure that our website was relevant to young people...people like myself, for instance?"

Given that this chap wouldn't see 40 again without the aid of a radio-telescope, if I were the interviewee I think I would have burst out laughing. That this young bloke didn't shows that they're made of sterner stuff in Stoke (or Hanley). I hope he got the job!

The Beat Goes On

A radio programme the other day featured one Dr. Julia Jones discussing her research, which suggested that, despite being told by their parents and grandparents that it would never last, the generations of music lovers from the 1950s onwards seem to have stuck with the rather broad genre of pop/rock in all its forms. These generations have continued to attend concerts and festivals and the proof of their continued support, and purchasing power, can be seen by such unlikely acts as Tom Jones and Lionel Richie headlining at Glastonbury. Dr. Jones conducted her research on the longevity of musical tastes by asking people about the first record they ever bought. This, and a couple of other things, got me thinking.

One of those 'other things' was Sheridan Smith's portrayal of Cilla Black, which has recently been repeated. I was a little too young to take any part in the explosion of musical talent in the early 1960s, but I thought these programmes encapsulated just how exciting it must have been to be part of the Mersey Beat phenomenon. I should think that anyone who could string three chords together must have stood a chance of being caught up in the music business and, in all probability, making a living, if not a fortune. Indeed, many of the artists from those days are still touring now. How different from today, where the principal route to stardom seems to be appearing on a reality show and attempting to fit 16 notes into a word where only one would do just fine (what I would call the 'Whitney Houston' effect, only the late Ms. Houston could do it well).

Simple tunes, played and sung with verve and feeling, became the background music to everyone's life. The early 1960s, when all of this wonderful music was pouring out of Liverpool, and elsewhere, was when I first started to purchase records. I can remember the early 1960s quite well, which they always say is a sign that you weren't enjoying the era with quite the same intensity as everyone else. As I was only 10 or so at the time, I was a bit limited in scope for anything likely to destroy the brain cells (unless you count wine gums) but I do recall the rivalry between those who were fans of The Beatles and those whose musical tastes were more rugged and supported The Rolling Stones. In order to annoy my female cousins, who were Beatles fans to a girl, I affected a liking for The Stones, but my heart wasn't really in it.

All of the above has been on my mind as I've been involved in an ongoing project to convert my vinyl records into digital files. This process has tended to reveal that my musical tastes have been eclectic, to put it mildly. Rammed together in the record box, the likes of Len Barry and The Supremes sit uneasily with Billy Cotton and his Band and The Bachelors. I also discovered a batch of records purchased in the 1970s, which I know was when fashion died but I didn't realise that music was on life-support too. My 1970s selection included 'Your Baby Ain't Your Baby Anymore', 'Chirpy, Chirpy, Cheep, Cheep', and 'Sugar Baby Love', amongst others too dreadful to name.

This brings me back to Dr. Jones' research question, in particular, the difficulty I would have in answering it. You see, in 1964 when I invested a goodly chunk of pocket money in my first vinyl purchase, I could have boosted my 'street cred' enormously by buying one of The Beatles' early hits, or perhaps either of Cilla's first number ones. I could have really gone for it with The Animals 'House of the Rising Sun' or The Stones' 'Little Red Rooster', but no. What did my ten-year-old self choose as the defining record to start my collection? A twee little ditty by Peter and Gordon called 'Nobody I Know'! The only saving grace, as I've just discovered, is that at least it was written by Lennon & McCartney.

Don't call me, Dr. Jones, I'll call you.

There's a concept known as 'magical thinking' which, if I've got this right, means that you believe that what you think and feel has a direct effect on reality. This article touches on that concept via the medium of the long-running U.K. radio soap 'The Archers':

Don't Give Me That Old Soap!

Have you ever found yourself thinking "Oh, please don't say that, it'll only make the worst possible thing happen!"? If so, you may well be suffering from 'Soap Syndrome'.

You see, I have this theory that we have become so conditioned by Soaps that we have come to believe that the way they work is actually how real life works. This is hardly surprising given the considerable blurring of the lines between reality and fiction that occurs in the world of entertainment today. Otherwise how do you explain such oddities as The Only Way Is Essex and Made in Chelsea?

You know how it is in Soaps, if there's a major celebration under way, somewhere, then you can guarantee that some appalling tragedy is taking place *at exactly the same time,* only yards away, thus handily counterpointing any possible feelings of joy and happiness which you, and the characters, might have been harbouring.

The same is true of any expressions of hope and optimism by one of the characters. We all know if someone says

"*You know, I think things are really starting to go our way*", that's the cue for despair, death and despondency to come winging their way, almost as soon as the words are out of their mouths. There are also some characters for whom the scriptwriters seem to take a particular joy in heaping misery upon, such people as Billy in Eastenders and Marlon in Emmerdale. Not that I'm particularly up-to-date with all of this as we made a conscious decision to stop watching all Soaps a few years back, because we realised that this amounted to a couple of hours each day that we would never see again, and we were also getting unaccountably depressed and agitated about a bunch of people who really didn't matter at all. I can't say that I'm sorry to have left their miserable little lives behind and, from what I've seen of recent excerpts in the past few years, nothing much has changed.

I was reminded of this when listening to The Archers, last week. This is our one remaining Soap vice. As you know, The Archers is a long-running radio series which is alleged to be "an everyday story of country folk", although I have to say that I live in the country these days and if it was like this I think I'd move to the Bronx.

Anyway, the aged mother of one of the character's (Heather) was travelling down in the car of her daughter (Ruth) from the North-East of England to her daughter's farm in the Midlands. You knew the way things were going when she said "*I've got so much to look forward to...*", which is the soap actor's equivalent of saying '*Can I have my P45 please?*'. Apparently she was delighted to finally be leaving the care home she had been staying in, and issued the fateful words *"Eeh pet, I'm that looking forward to waking up, in me own bed, at Brookfield".*

Well, she might as well have put a gun to her head there and then and saved five minutes of programme time. I said to my long-suffering wife, "Well, that's it, she's going to snuff it" (I have a way with words). Sure enough, Ruth was on the phone to David (her equally long-suffering husband) "Daaaavid, it's me mum, I can't wake her up" (regular 'Archers' fans will know that Ruth's pronunciation of her beloved's name gets more elongated as the years go by). Two minutes later, Daaaavid had rushed to the hospital but it was too late...Heather had gone.

I'll bet the actors set off for the Job Centre as soon as they see anything remotely optimistic in their scripts, knowing it will only be a matter of time.

As I said at the start, I think all of this just promotes a sense that to express any hope or optimism is tantamount to calling on dark forces to rain down their worst on you, and it shouldn't be like that. Of course, calling your offspring Marlon or Billy *(similarly long-suffering characters in Emmerdale and Eastenders respectively)* might be asking for trouble.

Unfortunately, once a topic has entered my head, I find it difficult to let it go:

A Little Bit of Soap

In a previous epistle, I was fretting about what I termed the 'Soap Syndrome', which is the assumption that real life works in the same way as Soaps do, so that any expression of optimism or joy is immediately countered by some appalling tragedy. You might, of course, argue that your life works precisely on this basis, in which case I would strongly urge you to check for hidden T.V. cameras in your home.

This time, I wanted to discuss the opposite effect. In other words, how it is that things which are commonplace in reality, hardly ever happen in Soaps, such as these:

Watching T.V.

What do you spend most of your leisure time doing? Do you? Really? My word, you must have a good deal of stamina! Well, I would suggest that, for the rest of us, the answer would usually be 'watching T.V.' and there's nothing wrong with that. It is the principal leisure activity across the world, except apparently for you, sir and madam. Do Soap characters then spend their leisure time slumped on the sofa watching whatever? Nope. Only on very rare occasions do you see them in front of a T.V., and even then it's usually so that a group of them can be gathered together for a blazing row or an embarrassing revelation. In fact, you will be very lucky to spot a T.V. in most Soap homes at all. Ken Barlow's old home wouldn't have had room for one, you would have had to evict somebody to get a 50" LED HDTV in there. Instead of putting their feet up and watching television, Soap characters do that which most of us now don't do, which is...

Spending every available moment in the pub or café, or both

At a time when pubs are closing the length and breadth of the U.K. because of the rapid decline of the traditional boozer, both as an entity and as a person, it is still the case, in Soaps, that the local pub has a thriving trade at both lunchtime and in the evening. How they afford it is beyond me, not to mention the fact that most of them must be hopeless alcoholics by now. If they're not in the pub, then they're in the café shovelling down a Full English, or mooning miserably over a mug of tea. The reason for this, of course, is that the writers need the characters to interact with each other and they can't do this if they're sat at home watching the telly. Not to mention that (unless you're the Royle Family or Gogglebox) there's no real dramatic excitement in watching someone watch the television. Therefore, Soap characters are stuck in a time-warp where the pub is the focal point of their lives at exactly the same time as it is becoming increasingly less so in real life. Of course, this burgeoning trade has one benefit, which is...

No-one ever has to travel to work

I don't know if it is still the case, but the Rovers Return and the Queen Vic. often had up to three people behind the bar at any one time, even when this meant that they outnumbered the customers by three to one. This, mind you, at a time when most pubs are struggling to survive with just the owner and his/her partner working there. In fact, most Town Centre pubs probably have fewer staff at peak times than the Rovers and Queen V. have on a slack Monday lunchtime. Why is this? Because everyone in Soapland works about ten yards from where they live. Thus, every café, pub, shop, bookies and underwear manufacturer is hopelessly over-staffed because work has to be found for them all. Most streets and neighbourhoods die a complete death from about 09.00 until 15.00 because everyone has gone to work or school, but not in Soapland. Here, people roll out of bed into the café (to consume a Full English), stroll across to whichever local enterprise has been lumbered with their labour, knock off for a few pints at lunchtime, return to the enterprise for the afternoon before heading back to the pub for the rest of the night. With all of this alcohol consumption, you would think that there would be inevitable brain damage, and you would be right because...

No-one ever reminisces

For the very good reason that they know how ridiculous it would sound if they did.

"Do you remember Alf?"

"Alf?"

"Yes, you know. He shacked up with that girl, who turned out to be a bloke in drag, but it was all right in the end because he went through a gender reassignment programme."

"Who did?"

"Alf. They were very happy together and they adopted a string of kids of multiple ethnicities with various physical and mental challenges. That was before the tragedy, of course."

"Tragedy? Which tragedy? The one where the aeroplane exploded directly overhead and wiped out half the village, or the one where the train fell off the overhead line and wiped out half the street?"

No, not those tragedies. I mean when the gas pipeline they were laying exploded, due to the careless disposal of a cigarette end thrown away by someone who was, ironically, just about to give up, which wiped out most of the population in a three mile radius. That tragedy!"

"Oh, that one. Of course! That's how I came to lose my leg and ended up in a wheelchair, until I was fortunate enough to get a state-of-the-art bionic leg and now I can run marathons without a trace of a limp"

Of course, this limited memory store can be expanded, when necessary...

Just whistle, and they'll come to you

One advantage that Soap characters have over those of us in the real world, is that they are clairvoyant. This becomes apparent whenever they start to mention, repeatedly in conversation, the name of a character who left (or even died - death is no restriction to career development in Soaps) years ago. You can guarantee that, once this process is in motion, the character mentioned will turn up, out of the blue, often bearing no resemblance at all to the person who walked out (or died) years ago. Children particularly suffer from this phenomenon. Some cute child will be sent to bed or school, never to be seen or referred to again for months or years, and will then return looking like The Hunchback of Notre Dame's uglier brother, having suffered a change in character in the intervening period that has taken them from a bright little thing with a song on his/her lips and a good word for everyone, to a malevolent brute Hell bent on revenge for some imagined slight. Eventually he/she will be put to work, just across the road usually and often working for their parent, but in employment terms it will definitely be...

Some Dark Satanic Mill

I well remember a scene, years ago in Coronation Street, in which the unhinged girlfriend (who also happened to be a lawyer) of the shop-owner, took him to an Employment Tribunal. I have been to a few of these in my time, and I can guarantee you that they were nothing like this. She flounced around the room, disporting herself over the furniture (to demonstrate her magnificent physique and long legs), giving lengthy speeches and making wild and unsubstantiated observations. Meanwhile, the members of the Tribunal looked on in helpless misery, apparently powerless to stop her antics. I fell off my chair laughing, which probably wasn't the reaction they were aiming for. Of course, the fact that she attempted to enforce her employment rights at all, even in such a bizarre way, was remarkable because most Soap characters don't seem to believe that they have any. At exactly the same time that the daily papers are screaming about 'political correctness gone mad' and 'worker wins massive payout for stubbing toe', or similar, the characters in Soaps are quite content to be dismissed without notice, for anything, work in incredibly unsafe and unhealthy conditions without complaint (until such time as a tragedy looks to be on the cards) and accept any amount of discrimination.

I know that Soaps could not possibly reflect the real world, in all its tedium and routine, and still be entertaining (although the Royle Family managed it) but some of the flights of fancy and dramatic clichés do tend to make you wish for a slightly better grip on reality. But, bless them, they're living in a time-warp that we seem to enjoy and perhaps long to be part of, at least some of the time. Gosh, look at the clock, I should be down the pub by now!

Wednesday on the Beach with Grandad

When my daughter suggested I could spend my birthday with her and our grandson whilst they were on holiday in Conwy, I jumped at the chance. It was only afterwards that it struck me how much my expectations of birthdays have changed over the years.

Not so long ago (or so it seems to me) the success, or otherwise, of my birthday would have been measured in the consumption of alcohol over the period. I should add that I still like a drink as much as the next man, or indeed the next woman as they apparently more than match the men drink for drink these days. Nowadays, my priorities have subtly shifted.

Of course, a trip to Conwy in the summertime is much like a trip anywhere in the U.K. at that time of year, something of a challenge. If the roadworks don't get you, then the traffic jams will. Sat-Navs that attempt to steer you around all of this can add to the stress. For example on our way home we had a picturesque detour around the outskirts of Wrexham, which added an hour to our journey and took several years off our lives.

The other problem with travelling in the summer is that so is everyone else and they invariably get to the car parks before you do. This is particularly an issue in ancient, walled towns like Conwy, which were never designed for off-street parking as the rebellious Welsh hordes of Owain Glyndŵr rarely turned up in their 4 x 4's.

Daughter and grandson were staying in a charming cottage about a minute's walk from the harbour. To while away the afternoon, Flynn wanted to go down to the beach. This sounds a bit grander than it actually is, consisting as it does of a few square yards of dubious sand right next to a jetty from which trips around the bay are launched.

I must admit I was delighted to see that, even in this age of Iphones and tablets, a few square yards of sand remain an attraction. There were loads of children and their parents down there. It was heartening to see that the British approach to the great outdoors was firmly entrenched, and that for every child in T-shirt and shorts (like Flynn) there were two others in sensible rainwear and jeans, prepared for all eventualities and temperature variations.

Flynn and I set about the business of building a sandcastle, which is a time-honoured tradition and one that was being followed by just about every child in our vicinity. Those who were not attempting to build a sandcastle were, instead, involving themselves in the other time-honoured tradition of burying one of their number up to the waist in sand. There is something wonderfully British about the sight of a child stoically enduring the application of wet sand to his/her nether regions, whilst wearing a rainproof jacket to protect those areas not yet covered in sand.

Building sandcastles on this beach proved to be a somewhat daunting task, as just a few shovelfuls quickly exposed a layer of stones underneath the beach which would have defied the best efforts of a man with a pneumatic drill. Nevertheless, we did our best with the limited resources available.

I'm delighted to say that I unconsciously found myself following in the grandad tradition. To start with, I was totally inappropriately dressed for the beach, having dressed earlier in the day with our later meal in a restaurant in mind. I was, therefore, caught between two stools. I wanted to be involved in construction duties but at the same time I was trying to actively avoid getting my clothing in a state. I felt like someone who had turned up at a building site in full evening dress. The upshot was that I was trying to dig whilst bending from the waist and keeping everything sand-related at arm's length, which was never going to be a success.

I nearly managed to pull a classic 'You've Been Framed' moment. Flynn wanted some water for the moat he was excavating and I was determined not to let him down, even though the path to the sea (well, estuary really) looked fraught with difficulty for someone who was trying to remain pristine. I gingerly trod a path over the most promisingly solid bits of sand, so that I was close enough to lean over to scoop up some water, without actually being in it. What I collected, as a consequence of the 'trips around the bay' fraternity, was probably two parts diesel to one part water but it was marginally better than nothing. Having collected my prize, I straightened up triumphantly, only to discover that one shoe had sunk significantly into the gunk below and I was in severe danger of falling over backwards whilst hanging on for grim death to a bucketful of diluted petro-chemicals. As this would have rendered all my efforts to remain pristine somewhat pointless and as I didn't want to be seen as a complete berk in the eyes of my grandson, I fought ferociously to retain my balance and was able to return, upright and only slightly muddy, to the castle-building site with my tainted trophy.

Flynn eyed my watery contribution critically but apparently decided this was what you could expect if you sent a grandad to do a child's job. The 'water' was applied to the moat, whereupon it disappeared into the sand and was promptly buried, anyway, which was probably the best thing for it. All further water supplies were obtained by Flynn from a less obviously polluted source and I was detailed to maintain a 'watching brief', ensuring the construction remained free from passing vandals in his absence.

Flynn and friend collecting some less polluted water supplies

At the end of the day, I reflected on my birthday and realised just how much pleasure I had derived from a simple activity in really unlikely surroundings. It dawned on me that doing something ineffably silly with the people you love is far superior to doing something allegedly enjoyable, without them.

Now, where's my bucket and spade? I've got my shorts on this time and I'm ready to construct!

Grandad by Flynn (note the stubble!)

Many years ago, it suddenly struck me that it was highly unlikely that I would ever see Australia or New Zealand in my life time. I remember feeling rather aggrieved about this, for no apparent reason as I had never evinced a burning desire to go there. I think it was just that I had always assumed that I could go there, if I really wanted to, and then suddenly realised that time and money were running out and would probably prevent me from ever doing so. From then on, I determined that come Hell or high water, I was going to set foot on Australia and New Zealand and, in 2016, armed with the lump sum from my pension, I finally did!

Time Flies (But Not In Economy)

This is a story which begins at Manchester Airport and ends in a cat litter tray.

When I was recently in Sydney (see Wizard In Oz) I saw a souvenir that I really should have bought, as it is a perfect example of Australian humour. It was a snow globe containing something vaguely Australian within, but what amused me was the slogan underneath, which read "SYDNEY - IT'S A BLOODY LONG WAY'

It is a 'bloody long way'. 10,555 miles, as the crow flies, from Manchester to Sydney, although I would imagine most crows would have more sense. Unless you happen to be independently wealthy, this vast distance is likely to be travelled in the Economy section of your chosen airline. I live in the hope that more enlightened generations to follow will consign Economy class travel to the ranks of 'cruel and unusual punishment', but I doubt it. I once worked with a rather grand lady who travelled by air frequently on business and she told me "I never turn right when I board a 'plane". I pointed out to her that, if I did that on most of the 'planes on which I've flown, I would be sitting on the pilot's lap, but I don't think she grasped my point.

I suppose that 21 hours in an aircraft would be just about bearable if you could sleep through it, but I just can't. I'm acutely aware that there is 34,000 feet of absolutely nothing between me and terra firma and I don't find that a comforting thought before I drop off (which is an unfortunate term, under the circumstances). On the two occasions when exhaustion overtook me and I did nod off for a few blissful minutes, I was rudely awoken by being bashed over the head as someone walked down the aisle. Cat-swinging is not an option in Economy.

The other problem, in Economy, is dining. Not, necessarily, the quality of the food, although that can be variable, but the need to eat as if you are a praying mantis, elbows tucked in to avoid encroaching on your neighbour's personal space, wrists bent as if performing delicate surgery. Of course, as soon as the meal has been served, clear air turbulence will set in with a vengeance and you'll be lucky if you don't arrive at your destination wearing most of your dinner. Also, just as a matter of interest, if you're not allowed to bring sharp objects on to the aircraft (understandably) why are you then issued with metal knives, forks and spoons for your meal?

 Leaving to one side the cramped conditions, the duration of the flight and the difficulties in doing anything other than sitting in one place for hours on end, the thing that really messes with your head is the time difference. We left Manchester at about 08.00 for a 7 hour (ish) flight to Doha and arrived there at 18.00, because of the difference between UK and Qatar time. Boarding a 'plane to Sydney at 20.10 for a 14 hour (ish) flight, we arrived at Sydney at 18.05 the following day. By now, if you're like me, you're hopelessly confused, but travelling to New Zealand makes it worse. I had always thought of New Zealand as being to Australia what the Isle of Wight is to England. It isn't. It is, in fact, over 1300 miles away and you cross two time zones to get to it. So, by the time you get to NZ, you are two hours further adrift from U.K. time and figuring out when would be an appropriate time to ring home would require the insight of Stephen Hawking. To complicate matters further, whilst we were in NZ, they put the clocks forward one hour, as did the U.K. (but not, of course, on the same date). Coming back to the U.K., you inevitably gain back all of the hours you lost on the way out, so we left Sydney at 21.30 and arrived back at Manchester at 13.15 the following day, despite travelling for 23 hours. As a consequence, although I've had jet-lag before, I've never experienced anything like this.

On the day we returned, we decided to try to go to bed at roughly our normal time to attempt to get our body clocks back in some sort of order. We made a decent attempt but it became more and more difficult. You found that, if you allowed your eyes to close for more than a fraction of a second, you were instantly asleep. I knew that I had to give it up as a bad job when I heard a loud bang as I was cleaning out the cat litter tray (you don't get this sort of detail with Bill Bryson, do you?). The loud bang in question had been caused by my knee hitting the washing machine, as my leg gave way underneath me because I had fallen fast asleep in mid-shovel.

Now that's what I call jet-lag!

Giving The 'Rahlag' A Miss

They're a sociable bunch, the Australians.

I know that this is a sweeping generalisation, and I'm sure that Australia has its own share of misanthropes. It's just that I've never met any of them, yet.

Take the other night in our hotel bar. My wife and I were sitting, minding our own business, gazing at the rugby on the television but really watching the comings and goings in the bar and trying to get a feel of the Australian social culture. Another couple of about our age came in and sat not too far away from us. They were nursing a couple of green and brown concoctions which looked distinctly unappetising and I later learned rejoiced under the name of 'Tobleroonies'.

Now, in England, it would be entirely possible to spend an entire night within feet of someone else without ever acknowledging their existence but I had a feeling this wouldn't be the case in Sydney. Sure enough, after a short while they found a reason to say something to us and a conversation rapidly blossomed as they moved over to join us. I'm rubbish at being sociable, so I decided to do something useful and go and get some drinks. As I made my way back from the bar, a couple of blokes sitting at one of those high tables you sort of perch at stopped me and said, with a grin, "you wanna watch it mate, our mate's moving in on your missus" Indeed, a tall strapping bloke, who I recognised as being part of their group from the previous night, was sitting talking animatedly to my wife and the other two.

It turned out that Gary, as he was called, had been out on the town with his two mates and had clearly had a very convivial evening. I don't know if he was really trying to chat up my wife, although it would have been a nice vote of confidence if he was, but he was clearly in the mood for a natter and was greatly interested when we explained that we were here as tourists and only had a limited amount of time in which to enjoy the delights of Sydney. We said that we had been for a walk down to Darling Harbour and were pretty exhausted after that.

"Ah, you want to go to the rahlag" Gary announced, in a manner that brooked no argument. I did what the English do best, I tried to look as if I knew exactly what he meant whilst searching desperately in my memory for anything that would give me a clue. "I always used to go to the rahlag with my old man when I was a nipper, used to love it. All the animals and the stacks of fruit and veg." He continued with enthusiasm.

It was at this point that the penny dropped. I had been reading the local paper, largely because it was free, but also because I think you can learn a lot about a country from its local press. I remembered now that there was a feature about the ongoing Royal Agricultural Show currently taking place in Sydney, although I hadn't taken a great deal of notice of it.

"Nah, you don't want to go there" the woman of the couple chipped in, "it's boring. You want to go to Manly, it's got a great beach"

This prompted a spirited discussion about the relative merits of both attractions. Gary, it transpired, was on a three day 'jolly', along with his two mates (who were watching the conversation with interest from their perch on the table opposite) sponsored by their trade union. Ostensibly it was to attend a union conference, but I think the eating and, particularly, drinking side of it was principally what it was about.

We, politely, said that we would keep our options open re our plans for the next day and Gary staggered off to bed, apparently satisfied with a job well done. The other couple, who were in Sydney to visit their daughter who was about ten months pregnant and due any moment, laughed at the idea of anyone wishing to spend their precious holiday time at the 'rahlag' and extolled the delights of Manly.

The next day, we decided to take their advice and took the ferry from Circular Quay to Manly and had a brilliant time on a scorchingly hot autumn day. Back at the bar that evening, Gary came in looking a little sheepish and considerably more sober than the previous night.

On the Ferry to Manly

"What did you do today?" He asked. We shamefacedly admitted that we had gone to Manly.

"I don't blame you. It's a nice place." He agreed, "You wouldn't want to go to the rahlag, it's just animals and veg."

Wizard in Oz!

As I've already intimated, I rather like the Australians.

Obviously, I can't say that I like *all* Australians. I've only met a few, and those that I have met have been invariably providing a service or selling goods of some kind, so were hardly likely to be unlikeable, but still...

I suppose what I like most is their sense of humour, and that fact that they're not afraid to use it. Take this 'for instance'. We were in a pharmacy in Manly (a town which must have a sense of humour with a name like that). I had an irritating cough (I've got an irritating everything, but the cough was excelling itself) and my wife had digestive problems. We sought the advice of the pharmacist, who suggested a couple of remedies. My wife, who likes to relieve awkward situations with humour, said to her "What with his cough and my problems, we keep expecting people to spray us with something". Now in England, that would either have raised one of those artificial and pitying smiles which say 'poor old bugger, it's a shame really, but if I keep smiling she may go away of her own accord', or would have elicited no response whatsoever. Here, the pharmacist said, "Nah" as she rang up the items on the till, and waited a perfect beat before following with, "we'll just spray after you've gone."

I should, I suppose, explain that, at the time of writing, we're on a brief stop-over in Sydney prior to a cruise around New Zealand (which is the primary purpose of this holiday). Hence the visit to Manly, because everyone has said we should visit there even if we do nothing else. Even though one large Australian gentleman, with quite a few beers under his belt, made a very strong case for the Royal Australian Agricultural Show, which we declined.

Manly Beach

Coming back to the pervasiveness of humour, there's the adverts. In Sydney, there's an anti-litter campaign ongoing at the moment. All over the city, there are huge posters saying 'DON'T BE A TOSSER!' and, in slightly smaller letters, 'put it in the bin'. Brilliant! But can you imagine getting away with anything like that in the U.K.?

Or there are the road signs, which are probably not intended to be humorous, but get there anyway. At a particularly complex and busy junction in Sydney (and, I'm sure, elsewhere), involving multiple lanes winding around a city-centre block, there's a point where four lanes emerge from a blind bend. There's no entry to these lanes for oncoming traffic, but this might not be immediately obvious if you were unused to the traffic flows in the city, and were perplexed by the junction. About 20 yards down from the junction, along those four lanes and facing the oncoming traffic, there is a large red sign with white lettering which says 'WRONG WAY – GO BACK'. No diagrammatic sign or translation into other languages, just this stark warning in English. And if you can't read English? "Well, you'd better learn pretty sharpish, eh mate?" you can imagine would be the response.

It's the same robust attitude that informs the small print of a meal offer at a restaurant on the waterfront at Darling Harbour, which read 'This offer is not available on Bank Holidays, or any other day when we can't be bothered'.

Darling Harbour

Of course, sometimes the joke seems to be on the weary traveller. For example, Australians seem to have a somewhat ambivalent attitude to drinking alcohol. They seem quite keen on it, but in a sort of slightly guilt-ridden way. On Good Friday, I nipped down to the bar in our hotel for a quick pint (well, a 'schooner' actually, whatever that is. Whether you get a pint, or not, seems to be in the lap of the gods here). There were a number of people in the bar but I was surprised to find the door was locked. I tried it a number of times, thinking I had made a mistake, at which point the bar tender came over and unlocked it, saying he could let me in for a last drink if I liked. Another chap joined me (also English, recently arrived from Blighty and like all fellow-born Englishmen, pathetically grateful to be served anything by anybody). When this other chap asked about the early closure, the bar tender explained that they were not allowed to serve alcohol after midnight on Good Friday. We were now rather perplexed as the time was 22.05, so he went on to say that he needed the extra time to clear the place and do his paperwork! I asked if I could buy another beer to take up to my room (a pretty standard practice in most hotels) *but was told that I couldn't because it would have meant walking through the Reception area with it, which was an alcohol-free zone.* Honestly, you couldn't make it up. I thought the local populace might at least kick up a fuss about being ejected from a hotel bar at 22.10, but no, they all filed out meekly, as did I. Mind you, on our first night, they had shut off all of the draught beer pumps at 21.30, for no apparent reason, and that didn't elicit a word of protest either.

It's a funny old place, Australia.

In Search of the Flying Fox

If you recall, we've been on holiday and, in the time-honoured tradition of holiday-makers everywhere, I thought I would bore you all witless with it!

We were going on a cruise around New Zealand but we had a brief stopover in Sydney, Australia before we departed and I was determined to get as much out of that short time as possible. We had visited Darling Harbour (after a marathon walk from the CBD) and had discovered the brilliant ferries that potter out from Circular Quay to all points. We had given the Royal Agricultural Show a miss, despite the earnest entreaties of one of our Australian acquaintances, and had enjoyed some time around Manly Beach instead.

A Sydney Harbour Ferry at Circular Quay

On the last full day of our sojourn, I really wanted to tick a few more things off from my 'To Do' list for Australia. High on this list was getting a chance to see the Fruit Bats in the Royal Botanical Gardens. I had seen these on a number of British television shows and I really wanted the chance to see them in real life. Therefore, clutching my, by now rather tattered, street map of Sydney, we set off from Circular Quay railway station with the aim of finding the Royal Botanical Gardens.

I'm not really much of a gardener. By and large, I cut lawns and hack off branches as and when necessary, and that's about it. Therefore, the only element of real interest to me, in the Royal Botanical Gardens, was the Fruit Bats. That is not to detract from the wonder that is the RBG, it is a delightful oasis of peace, tranquillity and greenery in the heart of a busy, modern city, but I wanted to see the Fruit Bats. I'm nothing if not focused ;-)

Therefore, I was more than a bit put out when I spotted a sign which said that the entire colony had been moved in 2012 because they were ruining the trees! From my point of view, I wouldn't have cared less if they had taken a chain saw to them (the trees that is, not the Fruit Bats). Apparently, they have been split between various other colonies widely spread across the country, none of which were anywhere near us.

I, of course, did what any reasonable person would do, under the circumstances. I sulked.

Eventually, and after a good deal of "I don't believe it"ing and huffing and puffing, I decided to console myself with a cup of tea at the cafeteria. We managed to secure a table outside, even though it was very busy, and I trotted off to buy the teas. A young couple, complete with very tiny baby, and their friend visiting from England, were on the next table and came in at the same time to order an appetising range of food. I was quite envious, but we had had a pretty decent breakfast and we knew that the cruise would hardly be a weight-watchers' paradise, so we decided to do the sensible thing and wait until lunchtime.

Sitting outside, enjoying our tea and the sunshine, I was surprised to see some rather large birds plodding around the tables. This was one:

Apparently, it goes by the name of the Australian White Ibis. I was rather surprised to see something so apparently tropical in such a mundane setting.

The group on our next-door table were busily cooing over the new arrival. Mother seemed to have decided that she had more than fulfilled her duty by bringing the little tyke into the world, so Father seemed to be marked down for the bulk of the childcare duties. Accordingly, as it was apparent that the youngster needed a nappy change, Father was despatched to the facilities to put that in motion (as it were).

At the same time, the friend from England was sent off to the serving area to find out where the food was. It was somewhat unfortunate, therefore, that only the Mother was left at the table when the food arrived. I have to say, it looked really something. There were fries and salads and falafel burgers, and all in very generous portions.

Unfortunately, two of the Ibis decided to take this opportunity to, basically, mug her. They launched themselves at the table and what they didn't carry off wholesale, they stood in. Father's falafel burger was an early casualty of the raid and I could imagine how chuffed he would be on his return. The friend was aghast when she came back. No amount of frenzied flapping of arms disturbed the Ibis in their work and no-one seemed to want to get too close to them (they're rather big birds). The last we heard, as we made our excuses and left, was the Mother urging her friend to go back and claim a refund on the grounds that the birds had eaten their food. I didn't hold out a lot of hope for that.

In a way, I guess I did see my Flying Foxes. The Ibis are certainly as adept as any fox at pilfering food, and they can certainly fly. I would have loved to have seen the Father's face when he came back from a lengthy bout of mucky nappy changing. I'll bet the Paternity Leave doesn't last much longer!

Steak Pie

It was our 27th Wedding Anniversary the other week! Hmm? No, I quite agree, you don't get that for murder these days and no, I haven't heard that one before. What did we do? Well, I guess what any long-time married couple does. We spent a considerable amount of the day staring down a manhole in our garden. Well, actually, staring was the easy bit. Thrusting a high pressure hose down there, with all of the attendant blow-back, was slightly more problematic. You see, my good lady wife had convinced herself that there was something seriously wrong with our drainage and, as it turned out, she was absolutely right. That which should have been flowing away, was, instead, hanging around, which, I'm sure you'll agree, no-one wants.

Regrettably, repeated thrusts with the high-pressure hose had no effect, other than to stir up the evil brew and we began to contemplate writing the day off whilst we waited for an expensive specialist to come and sort it out for us. Just then, we noticed that our next-door neighbour was working in his garden and we asked him to check his manhole to see if all was well there, which unfortunately, it was. However, he is one of these handy chaps with all of the necessary gear and he asked if we would like him to pop over and give it a go with his set of rods, to which we readily agreed.

A number of rods later, it became depressingly apparent to him that any blockage was not, in fact, in our garden, but in his! Cue intense foraging which threw up a hitherto unknown manhole cunningly buried under the roots of a bush. After an intense period with a chainsaw, which meant the demise of said bush, the manhole was revealed and so was the blockage. Much strenuous thrusting with rods eventually led to a satisfying gurgling sound as days' worth of 'that which you would rather not have hanging around' headed off to pastures new, albeit pastures you wouldn't rush to gather lilacs in.

By now, a good chunk of the day had gone, along with any ideas of having a 'posh lunch' (which had been our original plan, before the sewage got in on the act). It was too late for a lunch of any quality, so we decided to go with what we were comfortable with and headed for a little cafe in a nearby town. Now, whenever we go to this cafe, I invariably have the all-day breakfast, which is good and great value. Today, however, I thought I would show that I was not a slave to convention. I would eschew the all-day breakfast and try something else, something daring! I noticed, on the Specials Board, that they had Steak Pie, Chips and Gravy and I decided to plump for this. "I will have Steak Pie, please" I announced to the young chap taking our order, to the considerable surprise of my wife.

"Ah" He responded "I'm not sure if we have any left, I'll just go and check"

My heart sank. From experience, whenever a waiter comes out with this phrase, it means 'I know damn well that we haven't got any but I'll pretend to go and check so I can shift the blame onto the invisible denizens of the kitchen'. Sure enough, after a few minutes, he returned and apologised but there was no Steak Pie to be had. Predictably, I reverted to the all-day breakfast but somehow felt cheated of my Steak Pie.

When we came to pay the bill a little later, we pointed out to the cashier that the Specials Board still sported the offer of Steak Pie, despite the absence of same, and we had heard a number of other putative diners enquiring about the Pie with similar results. Surely, we suggested, it would be prudent to remove the offending item from the Board? This caused a look of consternation on her part. Clearly, she had every hope that there might, indeed, be Steak Pie tomorrow, so would such a radical step as removing it from the Specials Board now, really be warranted? We paid our bill and left, but musing on it later (because I really don't have anything better to do with my time) it occurred to me that this was a motif for our time.

You see, it seems to me that there's a huge longing in the world for something that, not only isn't there, but probably never was. A sort of global Steak Pie. This longing is for a golden past, in which everything was just dandy and which has been ruined by all of this pesky modernity and stuff. If we could only go back to (pick an era of choice, could be 1950s America or 14th Century Persia, or any other time and geographic location) then everything would be great, again. Or not. The Steak Pie might still be there, as a forlorn hope, on the Specials Board of life but, like it or not, we've got the All-Day Breakfast and we need to make the most of it.

The Steak Pie Repeateth

Common sense should have told me not to revisit this experience, but since when was common sense any fun? We went back to the cafe and our conversation went something like this:

Mrs. W: "They've still got that steak pie on the Specials Board, do you think they'll have it this time?"

Me: "They must have, surely? Even they wouldn't leave it on the Specials all this time if they didn't have any"

Mrs. W: "Ok, we'll go for that then, shall we?"

Enter, stage left, a waitress.

Mrs. W: "Last time we came here we ordered the steak pie from the Specials, but you didn't have any"

Waitress: "Oh yes, I remember" (*very much doubt this, we're really not that memorable, but still...*)

Mrs. W: "Do you have any steak pies?"

Waitress: "Oh yes, I'm sure we do"

Mrs. W: "Ok, we'll have two steak pies, please"

The waitress vanished and we waited, with some trepidation, for her imminent return, steak-pieless. Time passed and we began to feel more confident, our conversation turned from the existence, or otherwise, of steak pies and moved on to more pleasant things. We settled into our seats and relaxed, anticipating our steak pies, when...

Waitress: "Erm..." (*you can see where this is going, can't you?*) "You're not going to believe this but I'm afraid we don't have any steak pies. Some sort of problem with the suppliers."

So, this wasn't the outcome of a frenetic morning of steak pie selling, nor a temporary glitch with the daily steak pie order. No, this was a 'problem with the suppliers' which sounded pretty chronic. Had it been the case that there had been no steak pies since our last visit? Was the absence of steak pies a permanent feature? If it was, why were they still included in the Specials Board?

What I want to know now is, is the Specials Board just an aspirational list, a review of the dishes they would like to serve one day? There's Plaice and Chips on there and I'd love to order it to see if that exists, only I'm not that keen on Plaice and, knowing my luck, it would turn up if I ordered it.

We finished up with the All-Day Breakfast again. I have a sneaking suspicion that that's all they actually cook and everything else is just a figment of their imagination. I'll let you know :-)

Steak Pie – In The Kitchen

It may have occurred to you, as it has just to me, 'What the dickens was the waitress doing in the kitchen all that time *after* we ordered our mythical steak pies?' In the absence of any facts, I've done what anyone else would do in the circumstances, and made something up:

Waitress: "Oh my God, Oh my God, you've got to help me!"

Chef: "Calm down, whatever's the matter?"

W: "It's the couple who've just come in downstairs"

C: (calmly stirring a pan of beans): "What about them?"

W: "They've only just been and gone and ordered the steak pie!"

C: "Not a problem, tell them we've sold out, that always does the trick"

W: "But, you don't understand. They came in a couple of weeks ago and that's what we told them then."

C: "So?"

W: "So! When they asked again this time, I told them we had them!"

C: "What!! Why did you do that?"

W: "I don't know. I guess I panicked. It's on the Specials Board after all"

C: "I know it's on the Specials Board, but that's just because we don't want to be seen as somewhere that just does breakfasts. We want to be seen as a smart, sophisticated, small restaurant, offering a range of attractive options."

W: "With chips."

C: "Well, yes, alright, with chips. But you know what our clientele's like"

W (rummaging through the cupboards): "Surely we must have a steak pie somewhere"

C: "We've never had a steak pie and you know it."

W (wailing): "What am I going to do?"

C (grabs her by the arms and looks deep into her eyes): "There's nothing for it, you're going to have to take a deep breath, calm down, and go back down there and tell them...tell them...we're having problems with our suppliers! Yes, that'll do."

W: "Do you think that'll work?

C: "'Course it will. They're British, they won't make a fuss. You go and tell them that, I'll start cooking their breakfasts."

I'm afraid, once I get my teeth into a topic, I find it difficult to let go, hence:

<u>Steak Pie On Wheels</u>

I've written quite a lot, just lately, about my doomed attempts to buy a steak pie from a local café. The continued absence of this comestible, despite it featuring prominently on the Specials Board, seems to me to be redolent of a societal longing for something that used to exist, but no longer does. Alternatively, it could just mean that they can't be *rsed to change the Specials Board.

Anyway, it seems to me that this 'steak pie' attitude to customer service can be found in lots of other places, for example…

The other day we had to go into Burton upon Trent to collect a second-hand car we had ordered for my wife. The reasons why we've had to buy a replacement vehicle for my wife (by which I don't mean that I'm having the car instead of her, although…) are sufficient to drive a relatively sane person barmy, so I won't go into them here, other than to invoke a specific curse on the person who knowingly sold a particularly lethal car to a young family. May he (and the person who gave it an MOT) rot in an exclusive circle of Hell.

We decided that it would hardly be environmentally friendly to drive into Burton and bring two cars home so, as we unusually had some time on our hands, we opted to take the bus for a change. I should point out, at this juncture, that, to the best of my knowledge and belief, there has only ever been one bus service running through our village and that goes, about once an hour, to Burton.

The only timetable we had was a few years old but we decided it should be a reasonable guide and so we presented ourselves at the nearest bus stop about ten minutes before the appointed time, and an hour and a half before the appointment made to collect the car. Burton is only a half-hour ride from our village.

Can I say here, I think it is a shame that in order to make bus-shelters more or less vandal-proof, they've also made them decidedly uncomfortable? The same is true on unmanned railway stations, where those tip-up seats allow you to perch precariously, but not sit properly. Mind you, I suppose it is an advance on the stainless steel hurdle that constituted bus-stops in my youth, against which you could lean or, if small enough, hang from like a monkey.

The bus arrived bang on time and we boarded. My wife has a bus pass but I don't, due to my relative youth (yes, I know it's hard to believe). She said to the driver, very clearly, "A single to Burton Town Centre, please" My wife prides herself on her clear diction, whereas I, apparently, mumble.

"You don't need to do that, now" the Driver replied, "you just have to touch your card against the scanner" So she did.

I followed and said, "Well, I need the same but I have to pay for mine" and he duly charged me £3.10 and issued me with a ticket. I thought that this was a bit steep but it's been years since I last caught a bus.

We settled down in our seats and prepared to enjoy the novelty of a bus ride. Actually, 'enjoy' might be rather over-egging the pudding. It has to be said that if you were hoping for the smooth and relatively silent glide of a coach, you would be somewhat disappointed. I think you could have had a more tranquil journey in the revolving section of a cement mixer.

After a while, my wife said "Shouldn't we have gone through Sudbury?" (our neighbouring village). "I thought so" I replied with my usual quick wit and ready repartee. "Perhaps they don't go there anymore?" She suggested. I shrugged my shoulders, my conversational capacity exhausted.

Our bus then joined the A50 and continued on its merry, bone-shaking way to Mickleover. By now we were looking at each other quizzically. No bus going to Burton would readily divert through Mickleover. I hauled my ticket out of my pocket and noted, for the first time, that it said

'Single to Derby'. It is, perhaps, worth noting that Derby is in exactly the opposite direction to Burton.

Still unwilling to accept the written evidence, and that of our own eyes, as we trundled around various Derbyshire villages, my wife asked another passenger where the bus was going, and she confirmed it was for Derby. As getting off in any of these villages would not guarantee the possibility of a bus back to Burton, we realised that we were trapped until we reached Derby City Centre.

"We'll get off at the Bus Station and catch another back to Burton" my wife decided. "Does this go to the Bus Station?" She asked our helpful fellow passenger, as we weaved around the streets of Derby. "I'm not sure that it does" came the less than helpful reply.

With the Bus Station in sight, we pressed the bell and the bus pulled up. The conversation with the Driver then went like this:

Wife: "Do you go to the Bus Station?"

Driver: "Oh no, we try to avoid it because it gets so busy" (foolish of us to imagine a bus actually using a Bus Station, obviously)

Wife: "We'll have to get off here then. I asked you for a single to Burton, you know?"

Driver (looking at us blankly): "Oh!"

As it was clear that this conversation was getting us nowhere, other than Derby City Centre, we got off and headed for the Bus Station with all haste. The haste was, actually, a little redundant as we had just witnessed the express, non-stop bus to Burton gliding serenely past us as we alighted from our previous instrument of torture. Sure enough, on entering the Bus Station, we learned that the next bus to Burton would depart in twenty minutes and would call at all of the little villages we had just, unwillingly, visited, plus a few more for good measure.

By the time we caught our new bus, it was well past the hour when we should have been collecting the car. One apologetic phone call to the garage later, and with me nearly £10 lighter in cumulative bus fares, we set off for another scenic tour of the more obscure villages of Derbyshire and Staffordshire, accompanied by the usual crashes, bangs and bone-shaking bounces that are such a fun feature of public road transport. Quite why they offer free wi-fi is beyond my comprehension, I should think it would be a minor miracle if you ever managed to get your finger anywhere near your touch screen without doing you, or your companion, a serious and possibly deeply embarrassing, injury.

When we finally dragged ourselves into the garage, weary, deafened and shaken to the core, we had been in almost permanent transit for a total of three hours in order to complete what should have been a fifteen mile journey.

So, if you're wondering why we need a second car when we have such a wonderful public transport service on our doorstep? Don't ask, just don't ask!

Just in case you're wondering, I popped in to the café the other day and it isn't on the Specials Board anymore!

Out of the mouths of babes...

A couple of weeks ago, I went on my annual Walking Weekend with "the Lads". I've mentioned before that this epithet is becoming more and more of a misnomer with every passing year. After all, I'm 63 and I'm the youngest!

"The Lads" - author is second from the right

Anyway, I was to be dropped off to join the other three but before that, we had to take our six-year-old grandson, Flynn, to school. I drove there and Hilary and Flynn got out of the car, with Hilary reminding Flynn to say goodbye to

Grandad as he was going away for the weekend. This obviously preyed on his mind because; having said goodbye he set off towards school with Hilary but then stopped, turned back and opened the passenger door:

"Grandad, you won't forget your hat, will you? It's on the back seat."

"No, thank you Flynn, I won't forget my hat."

Apparently satisfied with this response he marched off again, but three paces later he turned around and came back to the car:

"And you won't leave anything there, will you?"

"No, Flynn, I won't leave anything there."

Turns, marches three paces forward, stops and comes back:

"Because you do forget things, you know?"

"Yes, Flynn, I know I do forget things"

Having decided that he had done all that could be humanly done to keep me on the straight and narrow; he set off for school with a cheery wave.

I always knew that there would be a time when the role of parent/child would be somewhat reversed, but I must admit I hadn't quite expected it just yet :-)

THE

REST

A Tour of the Talbot

Over the years in which I have been writing these books and articles, I frequently hark back to the days when my family ran the New Talbot Hotel in Anglesey Road, Burton-on-Trent.   It's odd that I should remember so much about this period of our lives, which only lasted two and a half years in total, but it was such a dramatic change that I think it has left an indelible mark on my memory. I was, therefore, rather saddened to learn that the pub is currently closed and there is a planning application pending for it to be converted into apartments.

I know it is hypocritical of me to feel this way, as I haven't been near the place for years, but it still feels as if a formative chunk of my life is about to be erased. So, I thought this might be a good opportunity to take a guided tour around the pub, if you're up for it? Of necessity, this will have to be a virtual tour, but I'll buy you a virtual pint on the way round. This is also definitely not a tour of the pub as it is now but, instead, as it was in 1964, when we first moved in.

From the photograph, you will see those big double doors at the front. We're not going in that way. They lead straight in to the Bar, are not often used, and I'm not absolutely sure that there isn't a dartboard behind them (and we don't want any unintended piercings en route) so let's go in via the side door instead. It's just under that illuminated 'Marston's' sign that juts out from the wall, to the right of the parked car, just where that bloke in the picture seems to be heading.

Anyway, let's get into the pub. It's getting chilly out here. The big wooden outer door is open so we can let ourselves in through the windowed door in front of us with the brass latch. The sound of that brass latch falling can be heard all over the pub, when it's empty, so no-one could sneak in unawares.

We're now in the Passage. You'll notice the red tiled floor and you'll also notice that a lot of the tiles are still a little damp. This is because we've only just opened and the cleaners have not long finished their work. All of the floors had to be mopped each morning, and that took some time. It was because of this that I managed to get myself into the doghouse on the first morning I was here. I came downstairs to find my Nana Whiteland mopping the tiles furiously, in anticipation of opening for Saturday lunchtime. I was genuinely surprised to find my Nana helping out in this way and, in my innocence, and in a doomed effort to be funny, I said "Oh, are you the char then?" Apparently this was <u>not</u> the done thing to say, Nana was upset and I was taken to task by dad. Not a good start to my new life in a pub environment.

There's a small round table to our left, with a couple of chairs and then, directly in front of us, is the door to the bar serving area with its hatch for dispensing drinks to those in the Passage. Pubs, in those days, had little tribes of people who very much stuck to their chosen areas and there was a definite group who only ever used the Passage. Another factor was that pubs were very much a male bastion, particularly the Bar, so ladies, who would be part of a couple more often than not, tended to congregate either in the Smoke Room or the Passage. In the week, this would consist of a handful of people grouped around this table, but at the weekend, the Passage would be thronged from end to end.

You're Barred!

Now that we've seen the Passage, I thought we might turn left and go through the door into the Bar.

Our Bar is a long, rectangular room. The window above the parked car in the photo is at one end, and the room then runs along the entire front of the pub, to the left of the picture. The furniture is around the periphery of the room. Bench seating follows the wall and, at intervals in front of this, there are heavy rectangular dark wood topped tables with wrought iron legs and bases, supplemented with thick, dark wood, stools, many with a sort of 's' shaped cut-out section in the seat. The tables are primarily designed for the playing of pub games, predominantly dominoes and crib. Overall, there isn't much concession to the concept of comfort; they leave that sort of thing to those who frequent the Smoke Room.

If we cross the room to the bar counter, the first thing you will notice is the choice. There isn't much of it! From the beer engine pumps (no keg or electric pumps here) you can have Pedigree, Burton Bitter or Draught Mild. That's it. No Guinness, no lager, nothing. If you don't like bitter in all its forms, you are in for a thirsty night. There are bottles of stout, barley wine and other bottled beers, of course, but the majority of our customers will be drinking draught beer. This lack of choice relates to the old-fashioned Tied House system, whereby the tenant of the pub was required to buy just about everything from the brewery that owned the pub. This is a Marston's pub, so more or less everything we require in liquid form comes from that brewery. If they don't (or won't) stock it, neither do we.

Spirits are on the optics and the shelves behind. Some are branded but many are Marston's own brands which they blend and bottle themselves (their Brown Label whisky is particularly favoured). On the top shelves are the various liqueurs and fortified wines, some of which get regular usage, like Warninks Advocaat (much enjoyed with lemonade and lime as a Snowball) and Tia Maria. Others were here when we took the pub over and look likely to be still gathering dust when we leave, such as Green Goddess, a triangular shaped, violently green bottle of uncertain origin and content which always intrigued me, but not enough to want to find out what it tasted like.

Sweets, crisps, chocolate and cigarettes are not the sole preserve of the brewery and these are purchased from, and delivered by, the wholesaler. I always rather enjoyed unpacking the cigarettes from their box, removing them from their paper outers and stacking the cellophaned packets onto the shelf in neat lines. Not only did this appeal to my sense of order and neatness, but I absolutely loved the smell of the carefully packaged tobacco. This was probably not a good thing for a ten-year-old to enjoy but we all have our little foibles.

Mum had a habit, which most people seemed to like, of removing the cellophane and silver paper when someone ordered a packet of cigarettes. This not only shortened the time between them purchasing these and consuming the first one, but also reduced the amount of litter that had to be cleared from the ash trays and tables at the end of the session.

That's my mum and dad there, busily restocking the shelves of bottled beer, fruit juices and pop before the pub gets into full swing. This is not one of my favourite occupations as it involves hauling the heavy wooden crates (and they were all wooden in those days) either up the slippery and narrow cellar steps, or all the way from the storage rooms at the back of the pub. It's a dirty job and someone's got to do it - but not me today, as I'm taking you on this tour!

A Bar of Music

As the Bar is really the heart of the pub, I thought we might dawdle here for a little while longer.

The Bar was the only room in the pub that was in use, lunchtime and evening, seven days a week. The Smoke Room (which would now probably be called The Lounge) and the Passage would be pretty full on Friday and weekend evenings, but for the rest of the time it was just the Bar. Lunchtimes would see a particularly busy period from about 12.30 to 1.30, as people popped in from work to grab a pint and a cob or a packet of crisps.

In the 1960s, spending your lunchtime in the pub was not seen as the beginning of the slippery slope and was a regular occurrence for many. Quite what a couple of pints did for productivity in the afternoon was open to question, but that was the way it was.

Either side of this lunchtime rush, the Bar would be inhabited by a handful of regulars who whiled away their time there every day. Mostly, these would be pensioners and those who were 'between engagements'.

The one permanent fixture in the lunchtime programme was the 'school' of dominoes over in the far corner, just by the bar counter. Some of the participants changed, dependent upon availability, age and infirmity but there was one constant feature, and that was Horace. Horace always sat on the bench next to the bar counter but one seat away, so that he was within hailing distance of those serving him but didn't actually have to pass anything from or to the counter.

Horace was a tall, elderly gentleman with an imposing personality, who was very used to getting his own way. He ruled his 'school' with a rod of iron. His partners quaked in fear of his scathing criticisms during the post-mortem which followed each game. In the quiet times before and after the lunchtime rush, the Bar was most definitely Horace's territory. My dad had the measure of Horace from the beginning, but mum was a bit in awe of him at first, and I think she found lunchtimes something of a trial as she tried to cope with Horace's terse commands, sharp wit and sarcastic comments.

Gradually, mum's confidence grew and she found that she could 'give as good as she got'. She also discovered that Horace was not used to women answering back and that she could easily slap him down, if he became too crotchety, with just a well-timed remark.

She also discovered that he was a widower who lived a pretty lonely life, scratching along on his state pension, and for whom the lunchtime dominoes session must have been the highlight of his day. Over time, Horace and mum's relationship developed from a grudging regard to a real, albeit very understated, affection. Mum even cooked him a dinner from time to time which I was sent over with, to his house across the road, which he would receive with grudging thanks (but you could tell he was really pleased).

Nevertheless, the question of who ran the Bar at lunchtime was one that was a source of constant low-level warfare between Horace and my parents. The crunch really came when mum and dad decided to introduce some background music into the Bar. A new system, called Reditune, marketed by Rediffusion (who were better known for T.V. Rentals) was being marketed. This was essentially an eight-track cartridge (well before they became generally available) and pubs could rent the sound system along with a monthly supply of pre-recorded cartridges, which were delivered like a Book Club - some choices were made for you and others you could make yourself.

Horace was fiercely against the introduction of music, breaking into the church-like hush of the Bar at lunchtime, from the start. Mum set to work on gaining his approval by subtly selecting tapes with songs and tunes from his era. Despite his protestations and general harrumphing, we began to notice a new sound beginning to emerge each lunchtime.

Horace was humming!

A Peep Behind The Scenes

Let's leave Horace and his pals to their devices (they'll only start arguing about who should have played what, in a minute, anyway) and pop into one of the areas that is not usually open to the general public.

We're just going to walk behind the bar (look nonchalant and nobody will ask any questions) and make our way through this door here with the frosted glass panels, in the middle of the shelving on the back wall.

This is our living room and, just a bit further on, is the kitchen. You'll notice that the furnishing of this room seems somewhat sparse. That's because we've transferred our stuff from our cosy terraced house, further down Anglesey Road, to here and what filled the rooms there doesn't even get close to filling these. Therefore, we've got the two armchairs, which mum and dad have had since they were first married, positioned opposite each other by the fire on the left of the room, with a rug between them. Then, there's a huge gap before we come to our dining table and four chairs. Mum always used to moan that this table was far too large, but it doesn't look it now that it's in the middle of this room. To the right of the table, pressed up against the far wall, is our sideboard and in the far right-hand corner, there's the TV and our budgerigar in a cage on a stand. Just in front of the TV (but sufficiently far away so as not to get a lecture on how I might be 'ruining my eyes') is a dilapidated stuffed foot stool made of red and white plastic, my perch of choice. To the immediate left of the door we've just come through is my piano. If it looks a little forlorn, that's because it has to contend with me practicing on it once a week, if I can be frog-marched to the piano stool.

Even with all of our meagre possessions distributed around the room, it would still be possible to hold a dance without bumping into anything.

I mentioned the fire earlier, and this bears closer inspection. I don't know if our predecessors made much use of the living accommodation in this pub, given that so much of it was trapped in the previous century (which, in this case, was the 19th!). The fire is a good example. It is an original huge black-lead range, with an oven on one side of a roaring fire. We never really used this range for its actual purpose and it was on the top of mum's list for urgent modernisation. My favourite element of the range was the trivet. This was a heavy black metal grille which pivoted over the fire so that you could boil a kettle. We never used it for that, but I discovered it was brilliant for roasting chestnuts, which was something I could never do successfully on the 'normal' fire in our previous house. Of course, appeals to retain the range for this purpose alone fell on deaf ears.

It's unlikely that you would normally see much of this room if you were a customer in the pub. At best, you might get a quick glimpse if either of my parents were dashing through the door to fetch something from the kitchen, or if they were lingering in the doorway trying to grab a quick look at the T.V. during a lull. However, one group would be familiar with the room. These were the clutch of favoured friends who might be allowed to hang back after closing time on a Saturday for an after-hours drink and, possibly, a snack. This used to seriously hamper my late night television viewing, on the rare occasions when I had been allowed to stay up. Also, there's nothing worse than slightly inebriated adults when you're a stone-cold sober child!

If we carry on and go through that doorway ahead of us, we should find ourselves in the Kitchen.

As I said before, the previous occupants seemed to have left the living areas of the pub trapped in the 19th Century and nowhere was this more evident than the Kitchen when we first moved in. On the right is the door to the back yard and, next to that, a window looking out onto said yard. Beneath that, there's a Belfast-type sink which is all the rage again now, but was considered to be as old-fashioned as the hills, then. To the left of that was a positively Victorian water pump, covered in cobwebs, painted in green and red, which was no longer in use, but looked as if it could have sprung into action if necessary.

To the left were various cupboards, an oven, and our very own leap into modernity, a fridge! It may seem rather odd thing to be excited about, but we had never had one. I was absolutely entranced by the idea of having ice constantly available (not that I had ever needed it before) and looked forward to making my own ice lollies and, possibly, ice cream.

The thing that I really liked about having a fridge was that it made it much less likely that the milk would 'go off'. Mum and I had a constant battle about milk 'going off'. If my cup of tea had a sequence of white dots swirling around the surface, I would point out that this clearly meant that the milk was 'going off'. Mum would respond with "It's perfectly all right", which was denying the obvious, and then would get cross as I endeavoured to fish the offending dots out of the tea before drinking. A fridge meant this was one less area of potential conflict. Of course, the rationale for us having such a lavish purchase at all was that it was needed for keeping the supplies for catering for the various pub teams (darts, dominoes, crib). I didn't care, as long as I got ice lollies and dot-free tea.

The Kitchen was the scene of a rather odd incident on our first Sunday morning in the pub. Friday and Saturday had been very busy, as everyone came to take a look at the new couple running the place. Dad was therefore taking advantage of the later opening time (Noon) on Sunday to clean all the beer-pipes. Buckets and tubes abounded, along with the astringent smell of beer-pipe cleaning fluid. Dad was particularly keen to get everything right on this first occasion of 'flying solo' as the cleanliness of the pipes largely determined the subsequent quality of the draught beer.

We were surprised by a knock at the back door at around 10.30. There we found one of our regular customers, I'll call him Alf, looking a bit sheepish and asking to have a word with my dad. Dad was brought up from the cellar, somewhat annoyed by this interruption. It soon became clear that 'Alf' was in a bit of a state. A brewery labourer, he was used to 'having his beer' as soon as he got to work in the morning. If he wasn't working, he could at least get into the pub at opening time (10.30 then) but, on a Sunday, he had to wait until Noon and he just couldn't manage that. His entire body was shaking as he sat in our Living Room. Dad pointed out that all of the beer was off, as he was cleaning the pipes. The only thing we had was the beer that had been pulled through from last night, which was standing in a bucket. 'Alf' said anything would do and I remember dad having to help him to hold the glass as he downed the flat, stale dregs in one. The transformation was remarkable, he instantly looked and sounded better and could now survive until official opening time.

Inching Across the Yard

I thought we might take a step out through the back door, into the yard, and get a breath of fresh air.

Immediately outside the door is my rabbit hutch, containing Floppy, my very ill-named first pet from our former home in Anglesey Road. From his name, you would expect a lop-eared variety, which he wasn't. Quite why I chose that name, I have no idea, but I was eight years old at the time of purchase and presumably thought it was an appropriate name for a rabbit.

I often wonder what Floppy made of his transition from a quiet back yard, to one in which he must have had more viewers than some of the digital T.V. channels, what with the steady flow of people heading to the toilets and the inevitable clutch of kids whiling away the time with a bottle of pop and a packet of crisps as their parents consumed more adult fare inside.

Two elements of the above might surprise a modern audience. Firstly, that the toilets were outside and involved a trip across the yard, in all weathers, for both genders. I can't speak for the Ladies, but I do remember the Gents as being rather basic, essentially a wall with a gully and just one cubicle. Secondly, children were corralled in the back yard. Pubs in the 1960s were very much adults-only affairs by law, and woe-betide the landlord who allowed children on his premises. In winter, Dad would turn a blind eye to the odd child huddling just inside the rear door to the Passage, on the understanding that a visit by the Police would require the immediate ejection of said child into the yard. Seems a very odd state of affairs now, doesn't it?

One advantage my rabbit enjoyed at the pub, other than having the variety of a constant audience, was that once the pub was closed, we could shut off the back yard and give him, and the dogs, the run of the yard and the patch of grass that passed for a garden. Rabbits, being rabbits, this did mean that the 'lawn' took on the appearance of the Somme, as holes appeared everywhere, but he seemed to like it.

You may remember Penny, our blue roan cocker spaniel, who found railwaymen fatally attractive because she associated them with the chocolate they inevitably gave her on our weekly visits to the pub? Now, ensconced in a pub of her own, she could spend many happy hours working her way around the bar tracking down the 'soft touches' who would give her a tit-bit if she looked at them appealingly enough. Sadly, she was a little old lady by the time we moved to the pub and died after about 12 months there.

Penny, in her younger days

However, she had been joined at the pub by Jill, a yellow Labrador who was a failed gun dog. Dad was a sucker for a sob story and Jill came to us as a reject from a chap across the road who bred pedigree gun dogs. Judy, Jill's sister, was taking to the training without a problem, but Jill was afraid of loud noises (well, all noise actually), which is a bit of a drawback in a gun dog, so she had no future with her owner.

Jill (left) and Judy as pups

Jill at the front of the New Talbot

After Penny's demise, mum yearned for another spaniel, and so Jane came to join us as a puppy. She and Jill took over where Penny left off when it came to working the customers in the bar. I was a bit dubious about letting both of them, and the rabbit, out at the same time but my abiding memory is of calling the dogs in and seeing them, and Floppy, bounding toward me, and turning around, in unison, and bounding away again when they realised this meant they were going in.

Jane

Lounging in the Smoke Room

Let's go back inside and take a look at the Smoke Room.

The Smoke Room is on the left going up the Passage toward the Bar. I suppose, nowadays, the room would be classed as a Lounge. It had slightly more comfortable seating and I think it might have been carpeted. There was bench seating, which was padded and comfortable unlike the wooden benches in the Bar, all around the walls, along with padded stools and more contemporary tables. It was generally seen as somewhere you could bring your wife or girlfriend and, at the weekends, the room would be packed with couples having their regular 'night out'. The men probably had numerous 'nights out' in the pub on their own during the week, but the weekend was when they dressed up (suits and ties were the order of the day) and "brought the missus out".

Mum (on right) and the wife of one of Marston's Directors in the Smoke Room

The room was frequented by groups of people, who met every week. This led to a perplexing moment for mum on her first weekend of serving, when one chap appeared with a tray full of empties and asked for "a Mick and a Milly, a Doris and a Dan, a Madge and a Maurice..." and a whole series of other names. It transpired this was how they always ordered their drinks, but it rather depended on the server knowing who drank what, which mum didn't! She got the hang of it, eventually.

At the weekend, music was the main feature of the room. We had a resident, volunteer, pianist who entertained the crowd with sing-along standards. The room was usually packed, on Friday and Saturday nights, with couples belting out a selection of pre and post-war favourites. I often wonder why singing in pubs died out? I suppose the advent of juke boxes, background music and karaoke put paid to the 'Pack Up Your Troubles In Your Old Kit Bag' brigade, but it does seem a shame.

The piano was particularly interesting to me, as it was also a pianola. By the simple method of alternately pressing down two foot treadles, you could feed a punched roll of paper through the mechanism, which would then play a virtuoso piece on the piano. I could sit there and pretend that I was playing something rather grand, which was a million miles away from the halting hammering of my infrequent piano practice sessions, as those gathered in the Bar in the early evening could readily attest.

I'm sorry if the décor of the room came as a bit of a shock when we walked in. You may have noticed (I don't really see how you couldn't) the large depiction of the view from a Swiss Mountain Chalet on the left-hand wall, behind the piano. This is what Hilda Ogden would have described as a 'muriel' and I think she and Stan had something similar in their living room, which was just as striking and out of place. I'm afraid this is the inevitable outcome of letting my dad loose with the interior decoration. Quite how he was sold this, I really don't know, but I'll bet it was at the end of a good lunchtime session. The best that could be said is that it was arresting, in that it was huge and nearly photographic in appearance, but the connection between the view from a Swiss chalet and a Smoke Room in a backstreet pub in Burton was lost on most people.

Mum hated it and mention of it always evoked another of her pet hates - the décor of the front room in our previous house. This had also been father's choice and involved wallpaper featuring rows of fake bricks covering the bottom third of the walls. Mum loathed it from the start. For decades afterwards, the mention of decorating would inevitably evoke a tirade about "those awful bricks in our front room".

Down In The Cellar

From the Smoke Room, I'll take you into an area rarely seen by the general public, which is actually the 'nerve centre' of the pub. The Cellar!

As we come out of the Smoke Room, you'll notice a brown, undistinguished door under the stairs. This is normally firmly locked, but, as I happen to have the key we might as well take a look. You'll have to watch your head as the ceilings are rather low, throughout. My dad has to spend his time down here pretty much bent double, like a latter day Groucho Marx! Also, watch these steps, they're quite narrow with an awkward turn to the left at the bottom, and tend to be permanently damp.

So, here we are, in The Cellar. This is split into three rooms. The one on our immediate right, at the bottom of the stairs, is for our high-value goods, hence the wire mesh and the locking door. In here, we keep our spirits and fortified wines and liqueurs. If we had wine, it would be here as well, but this is the 1960s and people usually only have wine on Christmas Day, certainly not when they come out for a drink.

The next room, on our right, is the real hub of the whole thing. This is where we stillage the barrels of bitter and mild, which form the bulk of our sales. All of it is hand drawn by beer engines up to the bar directly above us. The stillages, or thralls, line the wall on the far right. At the end of the room, you can see a series of brick steps let into the far wall with a wooden rail on either side. This is for the beer deliveries. The hatch in the pavement above is opened and the barrels are rolled over to the hole and allowed to slide down the rails, onto a pig bag, and on into the cellar. Strictly speaking, the barrels are supposed to be lowered on ropes to control their slide, but time is of the essence and this is in the days before 'elf & safety' really took hold. A full barrel of beer, whether of wood or steel construction, is a pretty heavy item, so you can imagine the noise as these ricocheted around the room! It was certainly not somewhere to hang around if you valued keeping your limbs intact. Once dropped into the cellar, the draymen would usually give my dad a hand with getting the barrels up onto the thralls, chocked (wedged, to secure them) and pegged (a hard or soft peg in the top bung to allow the beer to 'work' – a secondary fermentation which allows cask conditioned ale to become sparkling and bright).

In the room to our left are cases of bottled ale of all descriptions; Guinness, Mackeson, Owd Rodger, Mello Stout along with the 'drinks for the ladies' like Pony (a British Sherry), Cherry 'B' and Babycham. There is also a huge pile of coke ready to feed our somewhat temperamental boiler. I quite liked stoking this, but it was complete pain if it ever went out, which it did with monotonous regularity.

I once got immersed in this and conveniently forgot that I was supposed to be doing my Geography homework. When I explained to the teacher the following day that I had been 'helping my dad in the cellar', armed with that capacity for wit and ready repartee for which teachers were noted, he immediately christened me 'Cellarman'. Not unsurprisingly, as this was my first year at Secondary School and this epithet followed me through the years, I did not shine at Geography.

For the purposes of the Derby Telegraph Bygones page, that was where our tour ended, although I did threaten to complete the story at some unspecified point in the future. This is that point...

Bedknobs and Clubrooms

Let's leave the damp and dark confines of the cellar and head upstairs. As you'll see, here at the end of the Passage, just before the door out into the yard, are a set of rather grand stairs which sweep up to the next floor. They're all dark wood (possibly Oak?) with a very impressive handrail that is about six to nine inches in width (it's the 1960s, we don't do metric) with swirls at the top and bottom. It's obviously a set of stairs that is more than just functional, these are stairs on which to make an entrance. I imagine they were designed in the way that they are because these stairs are not just for the use of the licensee and his family but are also for the public, as I'll explain shortly.

When I said that the stairs were clearly designed for making an entrance, I'm sure they would have been many years ago. Nowadays, I chiefly use them for making an exit, usually much to my embarrassment. You see, mum has decreed that I shouldn't change for bed in the frozen wasteland that constitutes 'upstairs' but that I should get into my pyjamas and dressing gown in the relative warmth of our living room, just off the Passage. This makes sense, from a practical point of view. I can sit and have my bedtime drink (Horlicks or something like that) in front of the fire and television. The downside to this arrangement is that I then have to make my way up to my bedroom via the Passage. In the week, this isn't much of a problem as there is hardly anyone there and I can usually scurry up the stairs without many people noticing. At the weekend, however, the Passage is usually packed solid and I have to force my way through the throng before making my way up the grand stairs to the jovial shouts of "Night, Pip!" from the revellers below.

At the top of the stairs, if we turn left, we can see the door to my bedroom opposite and to the left is my mum and dad's room. We can take a peek in there if you like. The room is quite full of their bedroom furniture from our old home in Anglesey Road but there's still plenty of spare space. The New Talbot rooms were built on a grand scale. What does draw the eye is an impressive old safe that looks as if it could withstand a direct nuclear strike. This is where the day's takings are kept prior to banking.

If we go across the corridor now to my bedroom, you'll note that it seems a bit empty. This is because the single bed, single wardrobe and chest of drawers from my previously small bedroom are somewhat lost in this vast chamber. There's a small rug beside the bed as a nod toward comfort but the rest of the floor is an expanse of linoleum which certainly tested your character on cold nights and mornings.

I'm also not entirely alone in here. I can well remember my surprise, when I was just getting into bed one evening, to see a brown and white mouse scuttling along the skirting board. I was so shocked that I unconsciously mimicked the cartoons I had watched for years and shot up vertically, landing on the bed. I'm also convinced that I'm not alone in another sense, but we'll come to that in a little while.

A later feature of my bedroom was something dad purchased from a second-hand shop he rather liked in Moor Street. He was always getting things from there, which would have been out of the question as new purchases. At one time, I had a Super 8 film projector which was rather fun but in my bedroom I possessed, for a while, a black and white portable T.V. When I say 'portable', I mean by the standards of the day. You could move it around, but you risked a hernia by doing so. I was given strict instructions that I was not to watch this before bedtime and certainly not after 'lights out' but what, in all honesty, did they think would happen? Naturally, I would sneak the T.V. on when my parents had gone downstairs and watch anything and everything that came on, only switching it off if I could hear my parents coming up stairs. The upshot of this was that I was getting nowhere near enough sleep and looked like what happens if you don't eat your greens!

If we come out of the bedroom now and turn left we'll see that the landing turns to the right. At the end of the landing there is the door to our very Victorian bathroom, the fittings from which would fetch a fortune now. Just to the left of the bathroom door there's another door with a peculiar sliding wooden piece at head height, about a foot square. This is the door to the Clubroom.

In the 1950s and 1960s, most pubs had a Clubroom of some sort. This was usually a room that could be hired out for functions such as wedding receptions, society meetings and so on. If we go in, you'll see what I mean. The first thing you'll notice is the sheer size of the place. The room runs the length of the pub, with windows at either end. To our right, there's a small bar serving area but otherwise the room is empty apart from some folding wooden tables and chairs. From week to week, the room gets used for two purposes.

Firstly, it is the home of our weekly prize bingo which draws an impressive audience of ladies of a certain age. These are the days when only properly licensed bingo halls can offer cash prizes for games, so everyone else has to make do with prize bingo. Our prizes come from the local cash and carry and vary from household items of unimaginable luxury such as ironing boards or plastic washing-up sets, to toys and things as we get nearer to Christmas. I remember that one year they had a red plastic pedal car which I really coveted. It really looked the business and I think it might even have had working lights! I did manage to get one sneaky run up and down the clubroom in it, but then the bloke who ran the bingo came in and reclaimed it, in some dudgeon. He was the sort of chap who was really ideal for bingo calling, quite handsome with a cheeky grin and a definite way with the ladies. I'm not sure which was the bigger draw, the bingo, the prizes, or him.

Secondly, the Clubroom is the home of our local branch of the Royal Antedeluvian Order of Buffaloes, or the Buffs as they were commonly known. This explains the 'buffalo' horns on the wall over there, although whether they were ever really attached to a buffalo at any time is open for some debate. The Buffs, if you haven't heard of them before (and I hadn't, until we moved to the pub) are a sort of poor-man's Freemasons, although they would probably object to that comparison. They have their rituals, their costumes and their hierarchy but they don't take themselves quite as seriously as the Masons and their meetings are largely an excuse for a good social evening with quite a consumption of ale along the way, or so it seemed to me. They do a lot of good work for charity and they tend to look after each other, if any of their members fall on hard times.

One aspect of the ritual element of a Buffs meeting relates to that sliding piece of wood in the door that I mentioned earlier. That is known as 'the tile', I believe, and it's guarded by a doorman who sits behind the door when the Buffs are in session. The idea being that to gain entrance, you need to give the secret knock whereupon the 'tile' is slid across and the doorman ascertains whether you're able to come in, or not. I got in trouble about this because, hanging out in my bedroom, I heard the 'secret knock' times without number and knew it like the back of my hand. Therefore, when my dad sent me up to find out what the Buffs wanted to order from the bar, it seemed obvious to me to give the 'secret knock'. This, however, was somewhat frowned upon, apparently, although it rather depended on how seriously the doorman on duty took the whole thing. Anyway, I was counselled against it, but it didn't stop me trying it out from time to time if they didn't answer to a conventional knock on the door.

The Clubroom was also called into use on certain annual occasions. Chief amongst these was the Flower and Produce Show run by our own Horticultural Society where there was fierce competition for the prizes on offer. The occasion when mum was chatting with the wife of one of Marston's Directors (see earlier photo) was because the Director in question had been pressed into service to judge the annual Flower Show. Another occasion which ran for a couple of years was when we invited the vicar of our local church, All Saints', to hold a Harvest Festival Service in our Clubroom. This was surprisingly well attended, although I should think that the proximity of the bar downstairs made it a more inviting proposition than the church itself, for many. One year, we had a magnificent display of bread cunningly baked in the shape of wheat sheaves which was the centrepiece of all of the produce on display. The next day was our Harvest Festival at school, and guess what I was able to take along? Needless to say, the 'wheat sheaves' were the centre of the display at school too and I earned a considerable amount of 'brownie points' for the donation.

The Clubroom in all its finery, dressed for the Flower and Vegetable Show

Mum (left) chatting with the Director's wife

Flower judging is a serious business – I think the chap on the right was

the bingo caller, but I could be wrong.

Looks like a Royal Party! Mum (centre) with the Director and his wife to the right

The New Talbot Horticultural Society in all their pomp. The gentleman with the partially blacked out spectacles was also our volunteer pianist in the Smoke Room

Let's leave the Clubroom now and head for the final part of our tour. Just opposite the door of the Clubroom, you'll see another flight of stairs, not quite as grand as the flight leading down to the Passage, but definitely of that ilk. These lead to our attics.

Up In The Attic

There's a sort of wooden stair-gate across the bottom of the stairs, leading up to the attic rooms, because these are not really open to the public anymore, unlike the Clubroom. Many years ago, and certainly long before our time, the New Talbot Hotel was actually a hotel and the rooms on the third floor were the hotel bedrooms. I've never been entirely comfortable up here in these rooms and this passage, from an earlier article called *'And things that go bump in the night...'* might go some way to explaining why:

"The New Talbot Hotel had been a true hotel decades before we took over and, as such, it featured what had been 6 guest bedrooms on the third floor of the building. These were accessed by means of a further flight of stairs that ran up to the third floor from the end of the landing on the second floor, just by the bathroom and opposite the door to the clubroom. These stairs, like much of the upstairs flooring, were linoleum covered and were separated from the rest of the pub by a latched gate. Nobody had used the rooms for years and they were mostly empty apart from one or two which were used for storage. Therefore it was somewhat surprising that, as I lay in my bed trying to get to sleep, with the sounds of merriment from the bar below me ringing in my ears, I could distinctly hear the steady footsteps of someone

moving around in the bedrooms above and the tap, tap, tap of claws on linoleum as what I took to be a dog made its way down the stairs from the attic. Naturally, I did what any intrepid child of 10 would do in those days – I hid under the bedclothes and hoped it would all go away (it's not much of a strategy but it's served me well over the years).

For the next two and a half years, the footsteps marching around the rooms above and the tap, tap, tap of the non-existent dog's footsteps down the stairs, became a regular feature of my night-time pre-sleep routine. After a while, I came to the conclusion that, whatever was going on up there clearly wasn't going to interfere with me down below and I became rather nonchalant about it all. Having said that, no power on this earth would have got me up in those attics after dark, either then or now. The strange thing is that I never mentioned any of this to my parents at the time or for years afterwards and I don't recall mentioning it to my friends either. When I did tell my parents, many years later, they were shocked to learn that I had endured this nightly experience without ever confiding in them."
(see <u>Crutches for Ducks</u>)

You see what I mean? I used to avoid going up to the attic rooms on my own, even in the hours of daylight if I could, but you're with me today so it shouldn't be a problem. There just seems to be an oppressive atmosphere up here, but it's probably a product of my over-active adolescent imagination.

Now that we're up here, there really isn't much to see. Most of the rooms are completely empty, consisting of just bare boards and a Victorian hearth that any interior designer would crawl across hot coals for now. One room usually had the instruments from whichever group was currently using the rooms to practice in. This was a perennial source of income and it always seemed to be a different group. The main blessing was that, parked up there on the third floor, they couldn't really be heard down in the public rooms. I found the set of drums had a magnetic pull on me and I would have dearly loved to have had a go (it's still something on my bucket list) but I was under strict instructions not to go anywhere near them, although the occasional flick of a cymbal might have happened, by accident of course, in passing.

Of the six rooms, we could only access five of them when we first moved in. This wasn't particularly a problem as we had no real intention of ever using any of them and, given my concerns about what may or may not have been going on up here at night, I had absolutely no interest in finding out what might be in the locked room. However, I made the mistake of telling my mates about the attic rooms and, in particular, about the locked room. My mates absolutely loved the private space afforded by the attic rooms and couldn't understand my reluctance to spend any time up there.

The locked room, of course, held an irresistible fascination for them and, before long, we found ourselves, armed with a bunch of keys that had come with the pub and clearly dated back years, at the room's door. This was a dark brown door with sort of stained glass insets, which made it impossible to see inside.

As I dithered at the back of the gang, and tried to encourage the idea of giving up and doing something else, the rest diligently tried each of the keys in turn but to no avail. I had a real foreboding about this room and definitely didn't want to know what was in it. As time went by my sense of something dark and dangerous being released just grew and grew, largely stoked by the over-active imagination I mentioned before.

After a while, it became clear that none of the keys we had, or had managed to find, were going to open the door. By this time, my dad had joined us and, as he was as big a kid as any of us when he wanted to be, he readily agreed when one of my mates suggested we should break the door down. A lot of thumping and crashing later, the door finally gave way and revealed...

Well, it was a bit of an anti-climax really. It would seem that the room had been locked shortly after the end of the last unpleasantness (WWII) and was crammed with paraphernalia relating to that time, including gas-masks and ARP helmets. Most of the space was taken by a huge collection of flags of all the nations, and I don't mean little flags to wave in the street as a procession goes by. These were the real deal, full-size flags of all the allies which I would imagine would have been hung from the pub during the Victory Celebrations. If it was today, I would have been down to the nearest 'Flog It!' valuation at a rate of knots, but then we just tried on a few gas-masks and helmets, waved the odd flag in a desultory sort of way and then put it all back where it came from. I think my compatriots had their heart set on at least a dead body or two, whereas I was expecting some form of nameless dread to spring out on us. Flags and gas-masks didn't quite cut it.

On a lighter note, my other abiding memory of the attic rooms was a performance that my friends and I put on. The background to this was my abiding love of American comic books and super-heroes in general, along with the appearance of the wonderful Adam West and Burt Ward 'Batman' TV series. All of this fired my imagination and I had been trying to put together my own comic strip. This was hampered somewhat by the fact that I can't draw for toffee but I did the best that I could and people were very kind about it.

This, in turn, led to my asking my redoubtable Auntie Vera if she could run up some super-hero costumes so that we could act out my characters. My memory of Auntie Vera is that she would huff and puff and point out all the difficulties inherent in whatever you had asked for, but secretly she rather enjoyed the challenge and would always rise to it. Some weeks later, she presented me with a set of super-hero costumes which, given the fact that she had never seen a super-hero in her life and had no interest in seeing one, were pretty damn good.

The outcome was a one-off performance in which my mates and I attempted to dramatise one of my stories from my putative comic strip. Some other friends and my long-suffering family were dragged in to watch this debacle which took place in the attic rooms. I seem to recall that it was rather long on action, after the style of the TV Batman (BAM, POW etc.) and woefully short of actual story but I think we all had a good time finally getting the chance to act out the things we had seen on paper and on screen.

Well, that concludes our tour of the Talbot for today, ladies and gentlemen. Please make your way down the stairs to the Bar where you'll find a complementary pint waiting for the gentlemen and a sweet sherry for the ladies. I'm sorry madam, what did you say? Wine?? Oh no, not for a good few years yet will you be able to purchase wine in a typical British pub. We could run to a Cherry B or possibly a Pony (the little drink with a big kick - remember? It was too, consisting of a whole schooner of 'British Sherry'. You wouldn't need too many of them to start a sing-song). Of course, if you wanted to thank your tour guide in the usual way...Oh, you don't. Oh well, please yourselves!

The New Talbot as it is today, no longer a pub and now converted into flats – but I see the attic rooms are still there!

Down In The Mouth

I really cannot understand why anyone would want to be a dentist! It can't be the easiest of occupations, can it? Spending your life trying to do complex things in a very limited space, with the very real possibility of being bitten at any moment, does not sound like my idea of fun (if it sounds like your idea of fun, then you should probably subscribe to a more specialist publication than this one). Moreover, it must be pretty rare to get the heartfelt thanks of a grateful patient.

I was reflecting on this the other day whilst having a crown fitted. No, I haven't finally been elevated to the royalty, although I am still awaiting the call. This was a dental crown, which became a necessity when a venerable and sizable filling of mine fell foul of a particularly determined toffee, leaving a significant gap on its departure.

In my childhood and youth, my relationship with dentists was somewhat sporadic, which probably goes some way to explaining the existence of the sizable filling in the first place. Your experience may well have been markedly different, but in our house a visit to the dentist was usually occasioned by some problem or other, rather than as a result of regular check-ups to ensure good dental hygiene.

The difficulty with this approach is that, inevitably those visits you do make tend to be full of procedures, trauma and pain (not necessarily in that order) which makes you less likely to book another visit at any point in the near future, thus ensuring that the next occasion will, again, bring its share of procedures etc, handily completing the vicious circle.

Given the above, it is hardly surprising that the first visit to the dentist that I can recall was one I made to the School Dentist. I'm pretty sure that this chap hung out in some cavernous rooms in the Education Buildings in Union Street, but I'm willing to accept that my memory may not be entirely correct.

I know that I went by myself, for reasons that escape me, and was less than happy to be the recipient of six fillings in one visit, without any form of anaesthetic (having never had a filling before in my life). I'm sure these fillings would have been pretty minor in the general scheme of things, but the whole experience did not endear dentistry to me.

As a family, we were probably a bit of a disappointment to the dental profession. To the best of my knowledge, my dad never visited a dentist in his life, with predictable results. He was always *going* to do so, of course, but somehow it never quite happened. Mum suffered from gingivitis and, therefore, had frequent visits to the dentist. Eventually, she succumbed to the prevailing view in the 1950s and 1960s that you would be better off 'having the whole lot out'. It seems remarkable nowadays, when the retention of natural teeth is seen as the main purpose of dentistry, but I can readily recall conversations with my grandmother and others in which natural teeth were regarded as a nuisance and false teeth were the only way forward.

I suppose the advent of the NHS had made this a possibility. False teeth provided a relief from chronic dental problems and were depressingly common. I've just looked this topic up on Wikipedia, and it says *"In 1968 37% of the population of England and Wales over the age of 16 had no natural teeth"* which, if correct, is a rather alarming statistic. The situation was apparently even worse in Scotland where 44% of over 15s had no natural teeth in 1972 *(https://en.wikipedia.org/wiki/NHS_dentistry#History, Accessed 02.03.16, if you're interested)*.

Mum must have taken the plunge in her mid-thirties, which seems ridiculous now but was not regarded as at all untoward then. I remember falling off the sofa with laughter the first time I saw her without any teeth, which was probably not the reaction she was hoping for and I still feel guilty about it now. In my defence, I would only have been about eight or nine years old.

Nigel Lawson is reported to have written that "the *NHS is the closest thing the English have to a religion*.", if this is so, I'm risking a charge of blasphemy here, but I've always been surprised that people accept without question that they have to pay for dental treatment, yet go purple and start to splutter if you suggest that the same should apply for any other element of the NHS. Doing my research again, dental charges were first introduced in 1951, and in the 1960s (when mum was making further trips to the dentist few and far between for her) were just £1 for all treatment other than dentures. It's a bit more expensive now (although £1 in 1961 would be worth £15.56 today - I can bore for England when I get going, you know) but the principle had at least been established. I suspect that, for the majority of working people, a visit to the dentist is far more common than a trip to the G.P., which is free. Therefore, twice a year they dutifully cough up £18.80 for a dental examination and think little of it. As a consequence, you can usually get appointments when you want them, are seen at the appointed time(ish) in modern, up-to-date consulting rooms and are generally treated as a valued customer rather than a minor irritation. Compare and contrast with your G.P.'s surgery. Just a thought!

Mum's dentist of choice was a chap named Brown who inhabited some rather brown (ironically) and dark consulting rooms at the top of a flight of stairs in a building two doors down into Station Street from High Street. I think the old Burton Trader office used to be on the ground floor many years ago (although not in the 1960s, when mum went there). It may, in fact, be a dentist's again now, in a pleasing bit of historical circularity. Mr.

Brown had acquired the (entirely unjustified, I'm sure) sobriquet of 'Butcher Brown', largely by those (like my dad) who never went anywhere near him. As you can imagine, this didn't elevate my confidence when it came to my turn to tread his gloomy staircase.

Brace Yourself!

The reason I was heading up these stairs was rooted (did you see what I did there?) in an earlier visit to the School Dentist.

There is something essentially cruel about adolescence, particularly in the way that it strikes some of us. We're happily plodding along as a slightly taller version of our formerly cute infant self, until the hormones kick in and everything goes haywire. A fortunate few come through this process as a much improved version, others are visited by near-biblical plagues of acne and boils, yet others (like myself) are simply reconfigured into a less attractive version with various unexpected additions, such as prominent front teeth.

I can't remember when I first noticed this problem. I do recall never being able to bite into an apple like everyone else, I always had to gnaw at one on the side of my mouth, but this never seemed to be a major issue   However, by my early teens, it was increasingly obvious that something had to be done. Mum and I sought the answer from the School Dental Clinic, now established in a much nicer establishment in Cross Street. This seemed to be largely staffed by student dentists learning the trade, but they were friendly types and appeared to know what they were doing.

Mum was convinced that my affliction was a sort of Divine Judgement for years of dedicated thumb-sucking and I had pretty much resigned myself to being outed as such by the dental profession, the subject of ridicule and ignominy. Therefore, I glumly awaited the outcome when my mum asked the question about what was causing my prominent front teeth. To my surprise, the dentist asked to look at my mum's mouth and carefully watched her swallowing action. He then pronounced that we both had the same swallowing action, which involved the tongue coming forward, and that this action, repeated countless times over a lifetime, was the culprit and not any amount of thumb-sucking.

Being vindicated in this way did not, however, change the prognosis. If my teeth were to be returned to their ideal position, a brace would need to be fitted and, to make room for them to be moved back, some teeth would have to be extracted. The idea of this filled me with horror. School was full of tales of dentists standing on your chest and tugging manfully at recalcitrant molars and I had no wish to be party to any of that, thank you.

The tooth extraction bit was not to be handled by the School Dentist but was farmed out to my own dental practitioner which, in the absence of me having such a person, was deemed to be my mum's dentist (now made redundant by her shiny new dentures), Mr. Brown (you see, I told you we would get there in the end!)

In those days, there were two ways of having an extraction. You could either have an injection into the gum to numb the affected area, or you could opt for a general anaesthetic. It seems amazing now that total anaesthesia was ever an option at all, anywhere other than in an operating theatre, but it was.

I had, and still have, an absolute horror of injections. Therefore, from my point of view, general anaesthesia had a lot going for it. Not only did it avoid an injection (I couldn't even begin to imagine the horror of an injection into my mouth!) but it also meant that I would be blissfully unaware of any tugging and pulling involved. I was particularly concerned about this as it occurred to me that there was nothing actually wrong with the teeth that were to be extracted and that they might be somewhat reluctant to vacate the premises.

There was just one day a week at Mr. Brown's when the anaesthetist was in attendance, so there was inevitably a bit of a wait before I could have the procedure, which was absolutely fine by me. The day eventually dawned, after a few weeks in which I had tried to forget all about it, and mum and I trooped up the dismal stairs to Mr. Brown's surgery.

The waiting room was filled with glum people awaiting their call into the inner sanctum. A number of these were children of about the same age as me, who may well have been there for much the same reason, I suppose. As each was called into the consulting room in turn, and were returned to the waiting room to recover, the room took on the appearance of an Army Field Hospital with various groggy individuals clutching bundles of tissues to their bleeding mouths. If I hadn't been apprehensive before, I certainly was by now.

Eventually, my turn came and I was ushered into the surgery. Two men greeted me. One seemed a relatively cheery chap, who was introduced as the anaesthetist. The second was Mr. Brown, who I recognised from visits with my mum. Mr. Brown was a short, stocky individual with, I seem to recall, gingery brown hair. His most impressive features were his arms which would have been the envy of Popeye. In fact, if Mr. Brown had appeared against Mick McManus on a Saturday afternoon, I felt sure he would have given him a run for his money.

In a state of high anxiety, and with mum confined to the waiting room, I climbed into the chair and awaited my fate. Mr. Brown had music playing in his surgery (I think it might have been the radio) presumably to smother the screams of the maimed and mortally wounded. Mum had told me of her experience of being anaesthetised for her major series of extractions. In her case, the tune playing as the anaesthetic took effect was 'Cuanto Le Gusta', and the repetitive chorus just kept on repeating ad nauseum as she drifted into unconsciousness. I couldn't tell you what was playing in my case, I was just aware of the pressure of the mask, the odd odour of the gas and a definite sense of things getting decidedly weird.

When I awoke again, some little time later, it was with a feeling of relief. I was urged to stay still for a while but my overriding aim was to get the hell out of that room before they decided to do anything else to me. As I stood unsteadily, on the footrest, the Receptionist/Dental Nurse hurried up to stop me careering about and I'm rather afraid that I spun round and caught her a glancing blow on the side of the face with my flailing arm. I was thus returned to the waiting room in a state of some disgrace.

A few weeks later, when the gums had healed somewhat, I returned to the school dentist to have the brace fitted. I don't know if you've ever had the joy of, what feels like a mouthful of metalwork shoving gently but firmly against your teeth, whilst the roof of your mouth cowers behind a plastic plate, but I don't recommend it as a fun pursuit.

Over the following months and years, I made frequent trips back to the School Dentist for regular adjustments until they finally declared my bite to be back where it should have been. Mum had thoughtfully arranged for the bulk of the dental work and brace fitting to take place during the school summer holidays, so that I wouldn't miss too much time away from class but also wouldn't be subject to quite as much ribbing.

Nevertheless, I had to return to school with my new oral hardware and, in common with schools everywhere, one thing that occurred early in the school year was the annual school photo.   Never my favourite occasion, this photography session was particularly to be dreaded. No-one will ever convince an adolescent that an oral brace is a good look, because it isn't, and it only enhances the teenage propensity for glumness and self-effacement. All of which goes some way to explain the following.   As Crimewatch used to say..."don't have nightmares"

Philip gamely trying to hide his brace

The Order of the Bath

I was thinking about you in the shower this morning.

Well, not *you* personally, obviously that would be rather weird and somewhat worrying. I was thinking about what to write for this article. Fortunately, my location gave me the perfect answer (it was me in the shower by the way, not you, just in case my opening sentence has led to any more confusion). I decided to hark back to some bathrooms I have known.

This may seem a fairly mundane topic but what spurred my interest was the realisation that my family have progressed in a somewhat counter-intuitive manner with regard to bathroom facilities. Let me explain.

Our first home was a comfortable terraced house in Anglesey Road, located in that terrace running between Oxford Street and Cambridge Street. This would, originally, have been a three-bedroomed property but some enterprising former owner had made a great leap forward (for the early 1950s, anyway) by converting the back bedroom into a, quite spacious, bathroom. Thus my early years were conditioned by the joy of an indoor toilet and the luxury of regular hot and foamy (thanks to Matey, the no-tears bath foam for children - do you remember that?) baths. Of course, me being me, I managed to curtail my enjoyment of the indoor toilet by developing a fixation that I needed to have hurtled downstairs before the toilet stopped flushing, or risk falling into the clutches of the evil Toilet Monster.

We did have an outside toilet too, which was in a block of two over to the right of our shared yard, but this didn't appeal much to me. After all, if you could have a Toilet Monster in the refined surroundings of our upstairs bathroom, goodness knows what might be lurking out there!

After ten years of this relative luxury, we moved to take on the tenancy of the New Talbot Hotel, also in Anglesey Road. Here we still had the luxury of our own bathroom and indoor toilet, whereas our customers had to make the trek across our back yard to the usual facilities. However, the sanitary ware looked as if it was the original suite installed in the 19th century. This would not have been entirely surprising, given that the kitchen still had a hand pump for drawing water, over the kitchen basin, albeit no longer functional. The toilet had a cistern near the ceiling and a long chain for activating the flush. The bath was a free-standing one that interior designers would walk over hot coals for now but which was incredibly dated in the 1960s.

After two and a half years of pub ownership, it became apparent that the business was not working 'necessarily to our advantage', to paraphrase the remarks of the Japanese Emperor when he announced defeat in WWII. We therefore found ourselves homeless (and penniless) and were fortunate to be able to move in with my paternal grandparents in Uxbridge Street.

Nana and Grandad Whiteland had had the good sense to install a bathroom in their terraced house some years before. In those days there were really two options for installing a bathroom, in a terraced house that had never been designed for such modernity. You could either sacrifice one of the bedrooms (as in our first house) or utilise the pantry and coal house at the end of the kitchen (which is what nana did). There were some drawbacks to this second approach. Firstly, the bathroom had three external walls and, being at the end of the property, tended to be pretty chilly in the winter. Secondly, the building regulations then required that there should be two doors between the kitchen and the bathroom/toilet. Achieving this in the limited space available tended to result in such idiocies as two doors separated by six inches of space, as in my nana's house. As a young child, I used to rather enjoy hiding in this space, but then I always have been a little odd!

Nana had views about the toilet arrangements in her house. For some unspecified reason, she took the view that the indoor toilet was for the females of the species and that me, dad and granddad should take our filthy habits to the outside toilet, which lurked at the end of the yard. This was just about ok in the daylight, but at night when there was no light apart from an occasional paraffin lamp, it was definitely a bridge too far.

Two and a half years later, we finally returned to a home of our own, when we were able to rent a property in South Broadway Street. This was another place that appeared to have been bypassed by most of the 20th century, but it was ours and that was the main thing. The landlord, whose name escapes me, had been left a handful of houses by some relative of his and, whilst he was quite content to collect the rents on a regular basis, he really did not want the hassle of having to bring the properties up to modern (for the 1970s anyway) rental standards. There was, therefore, an unspoken agreement that, as long as we tenants didn't pursue him for costly improvements (or any improvements at all, really) then he would leave the rents at the ludicrously low levels that had been in place when he inherited the houses. This was quite a mutually beneficial arrangement provided that you were not at all fussy about sanitary arrangements.

Neither of the two houses, owned by him in our terrace, had bathrooms nor proper running hot water. There was a rather dodgy gas Ascot heater that provided hot water for the kitchen sink and the toilet arrangements were housed in a separate building to the right of the shared yard (as in our first house) which consisted of a toilet at either end, separated by a covered area for the dustbins.

Nevertheless, it was a home of our own and everything else paled into insignificance against that fact.

As I grew older, and gymnastic contortions at the kitchen sink began to lose their appeal when it came to personal hygiene (not to mention the potential for embarrassment if visitors arrived unexpectedly). I decided to take the matter in hand and invested in a portable shower arrangement, which was really designed for those with touring caravans that had no on-board plumbing facilities.

This consisted of a fold-up heavy-duty plastic tray, a series of aluminium poles, a very floral shower curtain and a length of hose attached to a plastic flask with a stirrup pump type handle. At the other end of the hose was a shower head which was about the diameter of a ten pence piece. The idea was that you unfolded the plastic tray, assembled the aluminium rods into a frame that stood in the tray, slotted the shower curtain over the remaining four rods, which then slotted on to the top of the frame. The shower head fitted on to one of the upright rods. You then filled the flask with hot water and pumped for all you were worth in order to achieve enough pressure to send the water up the tube to the shower head.

I am not one of the most practical people on the planet and when I first tried assembling this in our living room (which was not a good idea in itself) there was considerable uttering of oaths, as the aluminium rods fell apart at a touch and refused to stay still long enough for me to slot the top piece on, complete with shower curtain. When I had finally achieved it, and stood back to admire the result, our cocker spaniel Jane plodded over, climbed through the curtain and settled down to sleep in the tray. She clearly thought that I had kindly provided her with a four-poster bed.

Mum (left), Jane and Auntie Vera (right)

I think you can probably imagine the difficulties of using this Heath-Robinson arrangement. Even fully pumped, the resultant shower was weak to the point of being virtually pointless. Of course, the pressure never lasted enough for a complete shower and either the participant had to lean out of the cubicle and pump vigorously, or ask someone to do it for them. Moreover, after each ablution, the tray had to be emptied, which involved a degree of bailing followed by a careful elevation of the tray to sink height for the final few inches of water to be emptied away. All in all, it wasn't a relaxing process.

Don't talk to me about 'the good old days'; I'll stick with right now, thanks very much!

This is another of the editorial columns the Derby Telegraph kindly let me provide:

The Green, Green Grass of Home

"Spring is sprung, the grass is riz..." and 'riz' it most certainly is, and will be until the nights start drawing in and the first frosts put a stop to it all. The grass being 'riz' wouldn't be an issue if we could just smile benignly and watch it wave gently in the breeze, but we can't. We feel compelled to hack it to within an inch of its life, on at least a weekly basis, and grass, being of a hardy and sporting nature, just keeps on coming right back for more of the same treatment.

I once read some research which indicated that the reason we feel compelled to reduce grass to verdant stubble, in this manner, is because of our prehistoric forebears. Back on the savannahs in Africa, they relished the closely cropped grassland all around them as it meant that they could spot a predator from miles away, thus making popping down for a swift one at the waterhole less of a fraught exercise. Actually, saying that 'I read some research' makes it sound as if I spend my leisure time poring over academic reports when, in all likelihood, I probably got it from the back of a cereal packet, but it does have the ring of truth to it. Why else would we insist on surrounding ourselves with swathes of the green stuff which have no practical purpose? You might argue that a back lawn gives somewhere for the children and grandchildren to play, in the unlikely event of clement weather, and for dogs to do that which dogs must do, but what about those corner plots on the leafier estates which are cursed with large lawns, to the front and sides, with which nothing can be done at all other than to mow the stuff?

You may have gathered that I am not one of life's gardeners. Lawn mowing is, in fact, about the limit of my horticultural ability. When, years ago, I owned a flat, the lawn that came with it was more of a curse than a blessing. I used to put off the evil day of going to mow until I couldn't see my cat any more when he traversed the patch. With a heavy heart I would then attack it (the lawn, not the cat) with a strimmer (I didn't possess a mower) and reduce the patch to a series of stubbly hillocks for another month or so.

Harvey in the undergrowth of the garden of my flat, with my Capri in the distance

The strimmer, the electric rotary, the hover and all the rest of the motorised mowing paraphernalia are another reason why I dislike grass-cutting. There used to be something soporific and quintessentially British about the sound of a manual cylinder mower whirring along on a Sunday morning. It didn't intrude; in fact it enhanced the stillness of a summer's day. Now, in our neck of the woods, Sundays sound more like an industrial estate on piece-work. I'm sure you would get more tranquillity in a blast furnace.

Of course, it is easy to be hopelessly romantic about the old-fashioned mower. In reality, it had an unpleasant habit of stopping dead in its tracks, for no apparent reason, thus catching the unwary with a rather nasty blow from the handle to the solar plexus. This could have resulted in the shattering of the Sabbath stillness with a string of obscenities, if the breath hadn't been knocked completely out of the operator.

I'm not advocating concreting over our green and pleasant land. Well, not any more that we already seem to be doing. But wouldn't it be good if we could develop a strain of grass that grew to half an inch in height and then packed up? Perhaps we could genetically modify it with whichever gene is responsible for male pattern baldness, so that we could at least see some benefit from that? Alternatively, couldn't we, just for once, let the grass grow under our feet?

How Sweet To Be An Idiom

I used a phrase in a story the other day, which I thought was fairly commonplace, but someone commented that they were now going to add it to their lexicon. It made me realise just how much I rely on the use of idioms in my everyday speech, and in my writing.

Frankly, I blame Readers Digest. Whenever I was waiting, either at the Doctor's surgery or the Dentist's (and waiting used to be the main feature of the NHS) as a child I always used to make a bee-line (there's an idiom already) for the Readers Digest magazines, of which there were always a plentiful supply. I never used to read the articles very much, on the grounds that they might prove too long and I might have to depart for my appointment before completion (although, from experience, you would usually have ample scope for 'War and Peace' and still have time to kill). I usually read those little sections that contained jokes that readers had contributed or that section called something like 'Toward More Colourful Speech' which encouraged the use of idioms as a means of brightening the otherwise dull conversation of the typical Readers Digest subscriber (presumably).

I like idioms. I do think they add colour to any story. The trouble is that I pepper my speech (another one!) with them and this infiltrates my writing. All of my books have idioms as titles, largely because they are based on things my mum and dad used to say, which struck me as amusing as a child. I like saying "I'll go the foot of our stairs" to express surprise, even though it means nothing at all. I think the description of someone looking as if they had "lost a bob and found a tanner" perfectly sums up a hangdog expression, as well as being delightfully anachronistic. An old friend of our family used to say, of someone who was a little confused, that he didn't "know whether his a*se was bored or punched", which I thought was terrific. I'm sure every family has their own collection of such phrases, they sort of act as the family jargon - a mode of speech that everyone in the family instantly understands but which can confound (but also, hopefully, amuse) the stranger.

Where you really encounter potential difficulty, if you're as wedded to idioms as I am, is when you are trying to convey your meaning to someone for whom English is not their first language. Idioms are rarely a feature of formal language classes and, anyway, it would be impossible to learn all of the possibilities for every region of the country you are visiting. I found that, when I was teaching a class of students which comprised mainly non-U.K. citizens, I had to police my language carefully to remove any trace of the vernacular. Even so, I was always aware of a widening gulf of incomprehension. I remember one particular class, which consisted primarily of Chinese students, in which I became increasingly convinced that I was only getting through to a handful of the class. At the end of the session, I half-heartedly indicated the notes I had written up on the white board, summarising the key points of the lesson, and asked, without much hope, "Does that all sort of make sense to you?" This was the sort of vapid question I often asked of the U.K. students and they, being no strangers to the English concept of saying one thing and meaning another, would nod and smile brightly and, in all probability, leave the class none the wiser. In this instance, one particular student had been sitting on the front row and frowning at me throughout the lesson. When I asked my question, she answered firmly "No", which quite threw me as I'd never had that response before. At least it was honest and we spent the next 20 minutes or so trying to summarise the content of the three hour session in a manner that she could understand. I'm not sure that we succeeded.

Another time when idioms rather let me down was with my Subject Administrator at the time. Subject Administrators are the fine rain that falls upon the groves of academe which keeps knowledge burgeoning. Without them, the whole system would fall apart.

On this occasion, my invaluable assistant originated from Portugal and there were many times when I could see that we were not necessarily singing from the same hymn sheet (sorry!) On this particular day I had a number of interviews arranged with prospective students followed by an interview with a rather recalcitrant current student. Amazingly, all of the people booked for appointments actually turned up (quite a feat) which only left the recalcitrant student to be seen at the end of the day. As the Subject Administrator and I were walking up to the interview room, I remarked on how well the day had gone so far and then said, "We only need Sunshine *(meaning the student)* now to turn up and it will have been a good day" I knew immediately that we had wandered into the thickets of mutual incomprehension by the deepening frown on her face. She looked at me, and then stared outside at the darkening Nottingham skyline and said, very earnestly, "Yes, we *do* need sunshine." Which, I decided, was a statement you couldn't (and shouldn't) argue with.

This Green And Pleasant Land...Under Construction

I'm a NIMBY!

There, I've said it. For those who don't know this particular acronym, it stands for Not In My Back Yard and refers to those who object to any development in their neighbourhood.

Governments, both national and local, tend to refer to NIMBYs rather sneeringly, on the grounds that, if we had our way, there would be no development at all and, therefore, no new housing stock and industry in which our young people can live and work. I entirely accept this argument but it doesn't change my position one iota.

You see, in my opinion, to be a NIMBY is a perfectly economically rational position to hold. Why should we be expected to welcome any development which brings considerable short and medium term negative consequences, such as; loss of landscape or natural amenities, increased traffic, the noise and atmospheric pollution of building work, when the development typically confers little or no positive outcomes for those who already live in the area?

'Ah yes,' our political leaders would no doubt say, 'but that it is a selfish attitude. We need to think of the greater good of society.' Well, I would quite like to see what the reaction of Messrs. Cameron, Corbyn or Farron would be if you proposed to knock up a few starter homes on their respective back lawns. I doubt they would be quite so sanguine about it.

I'm particularly exercised about this at the moment for two reasons. Firstly, because our village is currently under siege by property developers. Apparently, our lack of a local plan (because of some bureaucratic nonsense) means that we are virtually powerless to stop any available land in the vicinity being concreted over in the near future. Currently, it looks like the population of our small village may well double.

Secondly, an article I wrote recently featured a picture of the offices of a company I worked for back in the 1970s. These had previously been the home of the Crescent Brewery in Burton upon Trent and were a fine example of brewery architecture. Yet the picture had been taken just before this building was demolished to make way for an anonymous and featureless warehouse. I had forgotten just how striking the original building was, until I saw the photograph, and I wondered how any planning authority worthy of the name could have allowed this piece of architectural vandalism to have taken place?

Harold Wesley's offices just prior to demolition

You might say that we should put our trust in the planning authorities, and I would say that you should consider taking more water with it. If you stop for a moment, in any reasonably sized town or city, and look at the range of buildings surrounding you, I think it's instructive to reflect that the mess before you hasn't grown organically, or happened by accident. It was actually *planned* to look like this. Highly qualified and well-trained people brought all of their expertise to bear to create this environment in which you are to live and work.

Equally, if your town centre is currently a wasteland of charity shops and pawnbrokers (and most are), remember that this is the result of a long term policy to encourage out of town development and discourage parking in town centres (or to earn as much money from it as possible). It isn't the result of forces beyond our elected leaders' control; it is the direct outcome of their policies down the years.

Tourists don't flock to admire the modern and clinical planning of places like Milton Keynes, they head to those places like York, Oxford and Cambridge which have retained their architectural heritage and the nooks and crannies of haphazard development over the centuries. Perhaps they know something our planners don't?

So, I'm a NIMBY. I don't want anything else in my immediate vicinity concreted over, thank you, and, even if I did, I would have no faith in the result being any improvement whatsoever on what has been lost in the process.

I think I'll go and lie down in a darkened room now. Can you shut the door and not make any noise please? I may be some time.

Born To Be Riled?

I wonder if, as a nation, we are becoming more belligerent? Before you ask, I absolutely include myself in this query. In particular, I wonder if those of us who, by reason of age and maturity, really should know better, including myself, are spending far more time than is healthy being hopping mad about something...anything!

You may recall that I gave an example of this phenomenon some time ago. I've spent many years following a particular group (The Enid, if you're interested) around the country. In that time, in some of their less popular incarnations, they have played some very dubious rooms in back-street boozers which have been attended by a varied mix of the populace, many in leather and/or punk type fashions. In all of that time, I have never witnessed any violence or threat of violence. However, the one time that I attended a Ken Dodd entertainment at Derby's (now cremated) Assembly Rooms, a fight broke out between two elderly blokes because one accused the other of pushing in front of him at the bar. They had to be separated by the Security staff.

I was reminded of that incident when I went to a local supermarket this weekend to return a faulty item. This was one of the 'cheaper end of the market' type supermarkets, which are, typically, leanly staffed and therefore don't have the luxury of a Customer Service Desk. We enquired about what we needed to do with this item of ours and were told to go to one of the check-outs, and an Assistant Manager would be called to deal with it, which we did. We knew this would be bound to cause delays to those using the check-out but there wasn't any alternative. One kind lady customer actually offered to let us go first, but we pointed out that it might take a little while and it was better if she completed her transaction.

The item was accepted back at the check-out without any difficulty and a Manager was called to advise on the correct procedure to be adopted with regard to reimbursement. None of this took very long at all, but inevitably a queue was beginning to build up behind us. As I had completed my part in the proceedings, by handing the bulky item over, I left my wife to complete the financial transaction and went to wait by the packing shelf. As she was collecting her receipt, I noticed that she seemed to be in animated conversation with a little bloke who was next in the queue. He was one of those grizzled sorts who could be anywhere between 40 (with a lot of worry) and 70. I decided to go over and asked "Is there a problem?" My wife explained that she had apologised to this bloke for the delay, but this didn't seem to be enough for him. He seemed to be of the impression that we had pushed in ahead of him in the queue and came up with some very complex explanation of how he had placed his items on the conveyor belt after my wife had arrived but before I had appeared with the item. I tried to explain the sequence of events as I saw them, but this clearly wasn't going to mollify him. I pointed out that my wife had apologised for his delay and that should be the end of the matter. We then set off to leave the shop.

Now, I know that common sense would say that we really should have kept on walking and drawn a line under an unfortunate experience. However, as we were walking away, he said, loudly for the benefit of the queue behind him "What a pathetic person!" This rather irked me. I should have thought that 'sticks and stones etc' but I felt this was hugely unfair and very unnecessary. Therefore, I walked back to where he was standing at the check-out, and said, quietly but firmly in his right ear "Don't"

Well, that did it as far as he was concerned. He was going to take me outside and visit violence upon me. I now did what I should have done in the first place and walked calmly away. Talking to my wife on the way out, it appeared that this chap had been humphing and muttering in the queue and she had made the mistake of apologising to him. This is always an error with the internally aggrieved as it gives them an excuse to enter into a conversation about whatever perceived injustice is aggravating them. Left to humph and mutter they will, in a perfect world, explode at some point and leave the world a happier place (once the bits have been swept away).

The rationale for this article is to confess my sins (I should have kept on walking) and to ask your forgiveness. It's also cathartic to get this off my chest because it has been bugging me ever since. I'm not a violent person by nature and tend to avoid confrontation wherever possible, I would certainly not expect to be put in such a situation on a Sunday morning visit to the supermarket, but I don't suppose either of those old blokes at the Ken Dodd concert went there for a punch-up either. Which brings me back to my initial question, are we becoming more belligerent? Please answer, using one side of the paper only.

Dogging My Footsteps

I've recently been tasked with walking my daughter's dog, Packham (my daughter has a fixation with the presenter of the same name) a lanky chocolate Labrador, so that he can do those things which a dog must do, without rendering the kitchen into a no-go zone. I'm only required if my daughter and husband's respective shifts mean that the dog is going to be incarcerated for the full day, but that's been happening a bit just lately, so Packham and I have been getting to know each other quite well.

Packham as a puppy

Our route normally takes us past the Stately Home that dominates their village. Between the road and the pavement, there is a grass verge and this seems to be his favoured spot for defecation. The other day, he had just completed his morning movement and I was poised to clear the mess up. Not, I must admit, my favourite occupation of all time but, in the immortal words of Arthur Guiterman:

"No matter what we are and who, Some duties everyone must do:"

Packham has an unfortunate habit of wandering as he dumps, despite my best efforts to stop this practice, so I'm poised with plastic bag in one hand, a supply of kitchen towel in the other and I'm steeling myself to deal with about a yard's worth of "ooh nasty" as Kenneth Williams used to say, when I notice a white car with a young couple in it drawing up to the pavement about 10 yards away.

My initial reaction was, 'I don't blame you for keeping as far away as possible' as it must have been fairly evident what I was up to. I was therefore more than a bit surprised when the car crawled along the road and came to a halt directly opposite where the dog and I were standing. There were no other cars parked in the vicinity, so there was no need for them to be close to my area of operation at all, and yet they had deliberately moved from a perfectly good spot to one that I wouldn't have been anywhere near, given the choice.

It was a hot day, and they sat chatting, with the window down, apparently oblivious of me, the dog, and the dog's recent evacuations just a couple of feet away from where they were sitting. I set about my allotted task as best I could, but the presence of an audience at such an intimate distance rather put me off my stride. Even the dog had the good grace to look embarrassed.

I couldn't, for the life of me, understand what would possess anyone to deliberately move closer to the scene of such devastation? Presumably, they were proposing to get out of the car at some point and this would, inevitably, involve the passenger stepping out onto the grass, exactly where the dog had just done his thing.

It is not possible, no matter how diligent the clearing, to remove every trace of defecation from a grass verge without digging up a cubic metre of grass and soil, which would soon lead to the whole area looking like the Somme after a particularly bad barrage. Therefore, it seemed to me, that the passenger could not hope to avoid a rather close encounter of the dog kind, that could have been easily averted!

To crib from Terry Wogan, "Is it me?"

Packham with his rosette (he won 'Dog with the waggiest tail')

A Line About Clothes

Is there anything more pointless than a man, trailing after his significant other, in a ladies-wear shop?

This question, amongst others, occurred to me one Sunday when I was doing just that. Don't get me wrong, I really don't mind this as an occasional occupation. It gives me the chance to observe and look around me blankly. I'm quite good at this. People often say to me, "what is it you're thinking about?" and refuse to believe me when I say "nothing". They can't accept it, but I am quite capable of just standing and staring. Walt Whitman would have been proud of me.

Anyway, back to my original contention. Other than providing moral support, I really don't see what is to be gained from having us in tow. We tend to stand there looking lost and not a little forlorn. One enterprising chap had brought along the Sunday papers and had arranged these along his forearm, like a sort of lectern, and was attempting to leaf through these as he trailed after his partner. It did mean that he had a tendency to bump into things as he went along, but you had to applaud the attempt to gain something from the experience.

You see, in my opinion, we're not really there to *do* anything. When I was young and foolish (well, considerably more foolish than I am now anyway) I had a tendency to make suggestions. Actually, I could have put that better. I realise that makes it sound as if I hung around the Changing Rooms with a bag of sweets and a disconcerting leer. What I meant was that I used to venture an occasional opinion. I quickly realised that this was not my purpose as I was invariably wrong. Well-meaning suggestions were dismissed out of hand or regarded as tantamount to an insult.

Ambivalence or, if the occasion calls for it, enthusiastic positivity are the name of the game. As time goes by, you become reasonably adept at spotting whether the prospective purchaser is;

(a) just going through the motions and is not really interested (cue ambivalence) or

(b) quite keen but needs confirmation (cue enthusiastic positivity).

Responding to (a) with enthusiastic positivity will only cause trouble. At best, you will be seen as an idiot without any taste whatsoever, whose opinions can and should be discarded. At worst, you will prompt the purchase of said item, which will be hated from the moment it arrives home and either promptly returned or left hanging in some dark, forgotten corner of the wardrobe as a silent reproach. In either event, you will not be allowed to forget it.

Oddly enough, the opposite situation works in an entirely different manner. If you are shopping for clothes and your loved one is with you, they are quite likely to have strong opinions and may even take over the whole process. Frankly, I'm quite relaxed about this. I hate shopping for clothes etc. and will put off the evil day until there really isn't any alternative. Men's' clothes and accessories are impossible to get excited about. Take shoes for example. If you're not a big fan of either black or brown, then you might as well give up. Trousers, shirts and tops have more options but here we have a tendency to buy things that either correspond to how we *used* to look, or how we would *like* to look. For example, today I saw a cheesecloth-type shirt with rolled up sleeves. Beside it was a picture of a slim, handsome, designer-stubbled, male model wearing said shirt and I realised that, in my mind, that was how I would like to look and that was why I was attracted to the shirt. The reality of me ever wearing anything like this would be too awful to contemplate. I might have got away with it forty years ago, although I doubt it would have done me any favours even then. Partners tend to guide us gently away from such fashion *faux-pas*.

Perhaps we need a male creche? Somewhere we could be left with a good book or today's newspaper so that we don't clutter up the shop but within sight of the shopper so that we can give a blank look or vigorous nod, as required, whenever necessary. I commend the idea to the house. Well, to the lady of the house.

Testing, testing...

I'm a fool to myself, I know, but a few months ago I accepted a jolly invitation from the NHS to have a five-yearly health check. I'm writing about this now because it only happened last week. You may wonder why it took months from acceptance to actuality, I certainly did. The reason I was given is that my Health Centre only does one a day, hence the lengthy waiting period. Why this should be, I have no idea. Presumably they have to go and lie down in a darkened room after each one.

I say that I'm a fool to myself because past experience should tell me that if you test for enough things, often enough, you're almost certainly going to find something, and this occasion was no different.

I tend not to visit my doctor very frequently because it can be a bit of a trying experience. The first thing you notice, whilst idling away time in the Waiting Room, is that everyone knows everyone else. It's a bit like a mini social club. The reason for this is that most of the people are there because they have a series of pre-booked appointments with the nurse or doctor. You often see people coming from their current appointment with a list of further appointments to book, along with a prescription that would gladden the heart of many a pharmaceutical representative.

This can be a little galling if you're an infrequent visitor and had an uphill battle to get an appointment in the first place. I don't know if it is the case at every surgery, but at ours there is little point in not feeling too well when you wake up and deciding to seek an appointment with the doctor for that day. If you're in the know, you will be well aware that to bag a same-day appointment, you need to start ringing the moment the surgery opens and keep hitting the redial button until you finally get through. If you are fortunate enough to get to talk to someone within the first ten minutes of this procedure, then you may have a chance of being seen, otherwise, forget it!

It seems incredible that appointments are divvied up on a 'fastest finger first' basis, but there we are. Hence the overwhelming presence in our Waiting Room of the chronically unwell and the permanently medicated, anyone else is only there as the result of a lottery.

I knew that a blood pressure check would be part of my evaluation and I also knew that it would probably be sky-high because of; anxiety about the whole process, nervousness about needles (a blood test was part of the fun) and general 'white coat syndrome' (the panic induced by being surrounded by people in white coats with the ability to do things to you). I therefore took the prudent approach of arriving armed with a series of blood pressure readings from the previous five days. Unfortunately, this proved to be counter-productive, not only was my reading at the health check, high, but so, apparently, were the readings from home. I was informed that I couldn't leave the surgery until my blood pressure had been checked by the duty doctor.

It's amazing how quickly you can go from relative equanimity to a shambling wreck. When I arrived at the surgery, I felt positively chipper, now I felt like I had been run over by a bus and yet, as my wife pointed out, nothing had actually changed.

Do you remember that old Stanley Holloway song 'My word you do look queer!'? Well, it was like that. I shuffled out of the Waiting Room, giving weak little smiles to those I passed as I clutched my prescription (having now joined the ranks of the permanently medicated) and a list of things I should give up, stop doing, or do less of.

Pardon, Nurse? Oh, thank you, yes, I think I might manage a little beef tea, and do you think you could plump my pillows whilst you're here?

So, and So

There are times, many of them in fact, when I wished I had paid more attention at school.

You see, I loved English as a subject. It was the only thing I was consistently good at. Or, I suppose I should say, it was the only thing at which I was consistently good, although I'm not sure that sounds correct either. And there we have the nub and gist of it. Whilst I really enjoyed English, the composition, the comprehension and the literature, I was bored witless by English grammar, which is why I can start a sentence with 'and' without turning a hair (not that I've got many to turn, anymore).

When the teacher was dragging some unfortunate sentence to the blackboard and ripping its grammatical entrails out, I was looking out of the window, or reading the next chapter in the text book. Verbs, adverbs, nouns and adjectives held no interest for me. I found metaphors and similes slightly more interesting, largely because I always found the standard example of a metaphor "The Headmaster flew down the corridor" such a wonderfully absurd image, redolent as it was in my imagination of a jauntily-worn mortar board and a billowing academic cloak, not that any of my Headmasters ever dressed like that but I did read a lot of Frank Richards' (who was actually called Charles Hamilton, I've just discovered. God bless t'internet!) books in my youth.

As a consequence of my foot-dragging as a child, I find it difficult to get on a high horse (you see, a metaphor already) about English usage and, particularly, abusage today, but don't imagine for a moment that this is going to stop me. The main difficulty I have is in using the right terminology to explain why I think something is wrong but, here goes, in no particular order:

1. Text – I hate the use of the word 'text' as a verb. It drives me up the wall (metaphor again) largely because it's so ungainly. "I texted him…" just sounds awful in my opinion and isn't noticeably easier than saying "I sent him a text". I know that I'm fighting a losing battle with this one and I also know that people will say that English is a living language and must be allowed to evolve. All of which is true but, in my opinion, there should be a difference between evolving and atrophying.

2. Breathe happy – this is but one example from many to be found in the media of a word being pressed into a usage for which it was never intended. Happy is not an adverb, happily is. If I had been paying attention at school, I should probably have been able to explain why this is just wrong on so many levels. You cannot, however hard you try, "breathe happy", but you might "breathe happily", unless, of course, you're currently in sewage treatment works.

3. Apps – some years ago, when I was adopting the mantle of a crusty old lecturer at my university, I used to criticise any student who used the term 'app' in their submission, when the correct word was clearly 'application'. I felt this was striking a blow for the eradication of text-speak from our formal language. However, as 'app' becomes ever more prevalent as an accepted term, I feel I have done my former students something of a disservice. Allied to this, we find 'emoticons' which may well turn up in an 'app' winking and grinning, although I note that even this term has now been superseded by 'emoji', the etymology of which completely escapes me. They must be doing well as I gather they now have their own film (or 'movie' if you insist, but I would rather you didn't).

4. "So…" – Finally, my absolute pet hate, which has become so ubiquitous that you can even hear respected academics using it. I'm referring here to the latest habit of starting every explanatory sentence with the word "So…" whether it needs it (it rarely does) or not. When I was grumbling about this to a learned friend of mine, he told me that people involved in public speaking are actually trained to do this to provide a moment to collect their thoughts before they embark on a sentence, without portraying that they are a complete imbecile by saying "Um…" or "Er…" or even "Half a tick…" or any variation on that theme. This I could just about accept if "So..." only cropped up before a sentence that had obviously been carefully considered and cunningly constructed, but it appears before any remark, no matter how asinine. Once you become aware of it, you hear it everywhere. Even those poor benighted souls for whom English is not a first language, will do it.

I think a line has to be drawn. I'm willing to concede, grudgingly, that "text" has become a verb, albeit a damned awkward one, and I'll even put up with "app" but I will never "breathe happy" as long as I have a breath left in my body and its more than high time to stop the so-and-so's starting every sentence with "so..." I wonder if one tactic might be to leap into the inevitable micro-pause which must occur after the commencing word "so..." with a lilting rendition of "...a needle pulling thread" after the style of Julie Andrews? I would try it but I just know the looks I'm going to get if I do. You could have a go, though. Let me know how you get on – perhaps I could visit you in hospital?

The Things You See...

'The camera never lies' we tell ourselves and that can be quite a comforting thought if the output of whatever you use to capture images (rarely an actual camera these days) happily accords with your view of the world, particularly your view of yourself but it can come as something of a shock if the image captured is more than somewhat at odds with what you expect. I had this experience, recently.

We were on a cruise. I know it must seem as if we always are but I assure you that isn't the case (although my waistline begs to differ). It was the first Gala Night and we were on our way to the Dining Room in what passes for our finery, me in a Dinner Jacket with dress shirt and black bow tie, my wife in a sparkly evening dress. To get to the Dining Room, it was necessary to pass through the Photography section, where a young lady was waylaying guests to have their photo taken. She asked us and I shook my head and passed firmly on, not because I dislike my photo being taken but because I know my wife hates the process. I was more than a bit surprised, therefore, when my wife said that, yes we would have our photo taken and I had to double back from my firm strides in the general direction of 'away' rather sheepishly.

We were duly arranged in a position, toes diagonally pointing at each other, our heads almost touching with me leaning down slightly in what I guess was intended to be a romantic pose. My wife pointed out to the photographer that she hated having her photo taken and had once had the result hidden by another on-board photographer to 'spare her feelings' (which, as you can imagine, did not really help with her irrational dislike). The photographer made the usual soothing noises but I noticed that she was looking at the results of her efforts on the screen of her digital camera, somewhat quizzically.

The following day, I jokingly said that we ought to, at least, gird our loins and have a look at the photograph, whilst all the time expecting it to be reasonably ok (as, indeed, was the one hidden by the other photographer). I don't think I have ever been so shocked as when I eventually found it. My wife looked fine, as always, albeit obviously a little uncomfortable. I, on the other hand, looked like Uncle Fester's less attractive brother and, from the lascivious grin I had adopted; I had designs on my good lady that would have been ruled out as too extreme by the authors of the 'Shades of Grey' series.

Needless to say, we didn't buy it. In fact, all I wanted to do was to get as far away from the hideous image as humanly possible. This was definitely unusual for me because I normally quite like having my picture taken, even if I'm not necessarily overjoyed with the eventual result. I think the problem is that we all have an image of ourselves firmly fixed in our minds and no amount of contradictory evidence can dislodge this. Photographs that correspond with this image, or get reasonably close, we approve of, whilst anything else is discounted.

For example, the picture I have used consistently as my 'author' photograph was taken at a studio session when I turned 50 (in 2004, if you must know) and I've always thought it was the best picture of me that I have ever seen simply because it fits perfectly with my imagined image of myself. What I tend to forget are the beneficial and healing effects of studio lighting combined with the artistry of a talented photographer versus the impact of the ravages of time over the intervening 13 years. The cruise ship picture made all of this very clear indeed.

My 50th birthday publicity shot

Most photographs of ourselves can be safely consigned to a long lost album in some forgotten drawer but, increasingly, there are some photos which live with us on a day-to-day basis, such as your Driving Licence, or your Buss Pass if you've reached an age when you have such benefits lavished upon you by a grateful local authority. These are, of course, a more recent phenomenon, made possible by the ease of capturing and printing digital images. In the past, the only photo that had the potential to follow you for a good part of your life was that stuck firmly inside your passport.

Today, your passport will last for a full ten years and has your photo printed on it, along with a microchip containing a whole tranche of personal identification information, including your inside leg measurement for all I know. But it was not always this way. Do you remember this?

Yes? Well done, full marks, it's a British Visitor's Passport. These were handy little documents you could apply for with the minimum of supporting documentation, originally at your friendly neighbourhood Labour Exchange but subsequently at major post offices. I must have visited the Labour Exchange for my first one, back in 1970, and I was probably served by one of my friends, as a number of them started their careers in the Civil Service there, but this was long before I knew them and I honestly can't remember the process.

The beauty of a British Visitor's Passport was that you presented yourself at the Labour Exchange/Post Office with the completed form, provided some means of identification and two black and white photographs of yourself (invariably the product of a photo booth) and the minimal fee of about £3, which was quite a lot then but was much less than a full passport and didn't involve anything like as much form-filling. Armed with this handy bit of cardboard, you were entitled to go and pester most of Europe, plus a few additional islands and territories, for the next 12 months. It was relatively quick, easy and hassle-free, so it's hardly surprising that it has been discontinued.

The downside of a British Visitor's Passport was the picture from the photo booth. I don't care how photogenic you consider yourself to be, photos from a booth always turned out looking as if you should be holding a prisoner number at chest height. I give you Exhibit A:

I've mentioned this awful image before, in 'Forty Years On' which you can find in that popular tome 'Crutches for Ducks'. This was 1971 and I had nipped into town from my summer job in the warehouse at Bovril/Marmite to get my passport photo at the Woolworth's photo booth prior to my first foreign holiday in Majorca. As you can see, from the photo, I'm dressed in my work clothes and, as I said in the original article *"I think it looks like someone wanted for questioning for Indecent Exposure...the expression on my face should give you a good indication of how much I was enjoying my vacation job."*

According to the section regarding the Exchange Control Act 1947 I had declared that I would be taking the heady amount of £30.00 out of the country with me, which I'm sure made the Bank of England tremble.

You would think, having been saddled with this disturbing image for a full twelve months, I would have made more of an effort for the next one, but apparently not:

As you will note, I have now moved up in the world and am now wearing a tie to denote my new-found clerical status at Harold Wesley Ltd. Other than that, nothing much has changed apart from an excess of facial hair, which was something of a feature of the 1970s.

I still look like someone the police would like to interview and the Blue Bird of Happiness has clearly avoided my nose at all costs. This was for my second visit to Majorca in 1973, about which you'll find more in <u>Back to the Balearics</u>, and I'm hauling a massive £49.27 to the Iberian Peninsula on this occasion.

My next trip to the photo booth didn't happen until 1981, when I began a series of trips to the Netherlands with my mate, Kev. I'd love to say this was an improvement, but...

Vaguely disturbing, isn't it? You certainly wouldn't want to meet me down a dark alley. I think the tie had belonged to my dad and I've a horrible suspicion that I may still have it. By now, the Exchange Control Act has long since gone and I could be hauling massive amounts of sterling off to the Low Countries if I wanted to, but I almost certainly did not as most of my available funds went to the Transport Club in Guild Street in grateful thanks for their supply of alcoholic beverages (which probably explains a great deal about my appearance).

By the time I came to purchase my fourth British Visitor's Passport in 1982, I was still haunted by this litany of faintly frightening images and determined to ensure that my next one would be a distinct improvement. I would take the time to go to a photo booth, properly attired and I would keep inserting coins until I had an image I could live with. Well, that was the plan.

I am, by this time, working for Marston, Thompson & Evershed, brewers of distinction. I always thought that working for Marston's was the ultimate reciprocal arrangement, because for years I had been donating all of my available funds to them in return for the supply of Pedigree bitter, so it now made sense that they should be providing the wages with which I could do that. It was something of a virtual circle, in my opinion.

However, some things never change and my ingrained habit of procrastination was fairly high on that list. I had known about my upcoming five day jaunt to Amsterdam with Kev and his brother for some weeks, if not months, but had done little in the way of preparation. Finally, it came to the Friday before we were due to drive to Harwich for our ferry on the Sunday. I took myself down to the General Post Office in New Street, Burton-on-Trent, to collect the form for my British Visitor's Passport, directly after finishing work at around 16.30.

I must admit, I was feeling pretty happy with life. I had a well paid and relatively undemanding job at a firm I absolutely loved. I had just broken up for a week's holiday in the exciting city of Amsterdam and I had managed to park my new acquisition, a white Ford Capri, right outside the Post Office. Yes, things were definitely looking up!

My beloved Ford Capri, complete with sheep – to be honest, it often looked as if I regularly carried sheep in it.

I presented myself at the counter and a bored-looking, but rather attractive, young lady and I had the following conversation:

Young Lady: "Yes sir, how can I help you?"

Me: "I'd like a British Visitors Passport form, please"

Y.L.: "Where are you going?"

Me (*chuffed that someone of the opposite gender is apparently taking an interest in me*): "Oh, me and a couple of friends are popping over to Amsterdam for a few days"

Y.L.: "When are you travelling?"

Me (*now convinced that she is definitely interested*): "We sail on Sunday"

Y.L. (*pushing BVP form through to me*): "Right, I'll need you to complete this form, provide me with two photographs and I will need to see your Birth Certificate"

Me: "Fine, I'll bring it all in tomorrow morning"

Y.L.: "We don't do BVPs on Saturdays"

You know, in books, where they talk about a cold hand gripping your vital organs? Well, I had that experience at this point. The time was now 17.05 and the General Post Office closed at 17.30 prompt. I was due to travel on Sunday and had no passport with which to do so.

Me: "WHAT??"

Y.L.: "You'll have to get it now and you'd better hurry up, we close at half past five you know?"

Me: "Right, I'll be straight back"

I have never moved so fast in all my life. The drive from New Street to South Broadway Street (my home, then) is just under a mile but it is all residential streets limited to 30 m.p.h. I have to admit that I did somewhat more than that figure in my headlong rush back home.

I hurtled into our house, scattering sister, dog and cat in my wake and screaming "Quick, where's my birth certificate?" at my bemused parents, which is not what you expect to be asked in such a peremptory manner by your first-born on a tranquil summer's afternoon.

The certificate was tracked down to an aged brown envelope in my mum's chest of drawers and I set off back to the General Post Office, risking life and limb, that of mine and everyone else, in the process.

It was 17.25 when I raced into the august portals of the GPO. The staff, in time-honoured public-sector fashion in the early 1980s, had their coats on and were waiting, underneath the clock, for the minutes to tick away so that they could go home for the weekend. This included the girl who had been dealing with me. Fortunately, she took pity on me and detached herself from the 'POETS' club (you know, Push Off Early, Tomorrow's Saturday...only it's not usually 'push') to reopen her counter.

Me: (*more than a bit breathlessly*) "Right, here's my birth certificate and my last British Vistor's Passport"

Y.L.: "Has anything changed since your last passport?"

Me: "No, I don't think so"

Y.L.: "Right, I'll fill in the form. You need to get your photos. There's a booth over there and be quick, we close in five minutes!"

So I threw myself into the booth, deposited the coin and resigned myself to whatever came out. With just seconds to spare, I ran to the counter with my still-drying photos. She attached one to the form and one to the passport. I paid my fee and thanked her profusely.

This was the result:

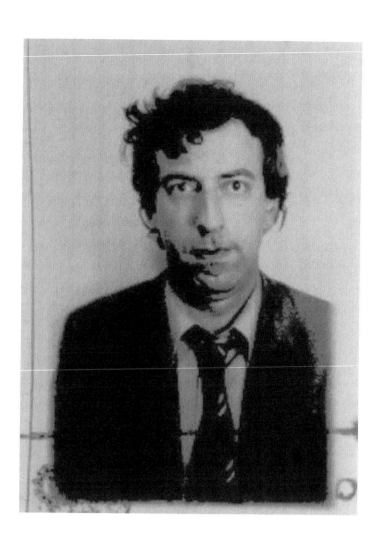

I think it pretty much failed to meet my ambitions on all counts. It's the only passport photo that I know of which has made a Passport Officer laugh out loud. In fact, he was so taken with it that he made a point of sharing it with his colleague in the next booth, and he dissolved into hysterical laughter, too.

Kev and his brother thought the whole thing was highly amusing, whereas it's taken a few years for me to see the funny side of it.

The camera might never lie, but you would think it could see it's way clear to the odd fib now and then, wouldn't you?

Mis-Shapes

Over the years, various manufacturers and suppliers have discovered that there is money to be made from selling that which they would have previously thrown away. In evidence, I would cite broken biscuits, chocolate mis-shapes and batter bits. It therefore struck me that this was a good excuse for using up one or two pieces I've written that really don't fit anywhere, hence this section. From time to time I get an idea for some sort of dumb joke in my head and, once it's there, I can't shift it until I've actually done something with it. All of which explains the following. They're not 'nostalgedy', but they've been kicking around in a dusty folder in my P.C. and I think it's time they saw the daylight. You might disagree ;-)

Audacious Auditions

Scene: A grubby and untidy back-street office. Behind a desk overflowing with newspaper cuttings, final demands, playbills and hopeful letters sits a balding, chubby man in an ill-fitting suit. On the wall behind him there is a sign bedecked with little stars and bearing the rather optimistic legend 'Wishaw's Theatrical Agency - wishes come true with Wishaw!' A middle-aged woman, dressed rather younger than her years in a figure-hugging sweater and jeans, pokes her head around the door:

Veronica: "You wanted to see me, Mr. Wishaw?"

Wishaw: "Veronica! Come on in"

V: "Thanks, Mr. Wishaw"

She wiggles toward a chair and clears a few papers off it in order to sit down.

V: "BTW, Mr. Wishaw, it's 'Veronique' now, I've changed it"

W: "Veronique eh? Very pretty, I'm sure. Now then, Veronica..."

V: "Veronique!"

W: "Yes, of course. Well, look V, it's like this. You know I sent you up for that gas boiler ad?"

V: "Yes, Mr. Wishaw. Thank you, Mr. Wishaw"

W: "Thanks are unnecessary, Veron...V. I've had a note back from the producer and I thought I ought to share it with you."

V: (*squeals excitedly*) "Oh, some notes! I'm always willing to learn, Mr. W."

W: "Well, not notes as such, V. You see, I sent you for that audition because I thought it was something you could do standing on your head. However, from what it says here, it seems that's exactly what you did do"

V: "That's right, Mr. Wishaw. You see, the shot was just from my feet up to my knees, and this animated corgi was going to be added in later. I couldn't see how I could convey the important emotions with just my feet and knees"

W: "So you stood on your head?"

V: "Yes, that's right. I wanted the viewer to understand the depth of my feelings"

W: "Let me get this straight, V. As I understand it, the nub and the gist of the ad is that a cartoon corgi brings a newspaper to you with a headline that shows that 1 in 11 boilers are potentially dangerous. Is that right?"

V: "That's it, Mr. W. It's an emotional subject. People could get hurt!"

W: "I don't doubt it, V. But don't you think the sight of you hanging upside down might just distract the viewers a tiny bit from the content of the ad?"

V: (*sulkily*) "I don't see why, Mr. Wishaw"

W: "Well, be that as it may, V. Leaving the 'standing on your head' approach to one side, for the moment, the other thing the producer was somewhat concerned about was your modification of your lines"

V: (*very sulkily*) "I don't think he properly understood my motivation"

W: "V. All he wanted you to say was 'Oh dear, corgi, that's not good is it?' and then the voiceover would explain the rest. But you didn't say that, did you V?"

V: (*moodlily*) "No, Mr. W."

W: "What you actually said was, and I quote, 'Good grief, my dog can read, I'm going to be rich beyond my wildest dreams!'"

V: "Well, that's what I would have said, Mr. W. I have to be true to my character, to my inner self."

Veronica slams her right hand to her chest for dramatic effect.

W: (*sympathetically*) "V, no-one doubts that your heart is in the right place. It's just that..."

Wishaw stares fixedly at Veronica's sagging embonpoint

W: (*distractedly*) "...your charley's aren't"

V: "I beg your pardon!"

W: (*hastily*) "Charlie's Aunt! There's talk of doing a run, thought you might fancy it?"

V: (*suspiciously*) "Where?"

Wishaw is still distracted and continues to stare at Veronica's chest

W: "God kn...Godalming!"

V: "I don't think so, Mr. W. It's not where I see myself right now. "

W: "What? Godalming?"

V: "No, silly! I mean my creative journey. Light comedy is so... yesterday. Today, I see myself as more...Ibsen, possibly Chekhov, Beckett perhaps?"

W: "Oh V! No, love. You mustn't run before you can walk." Picks up a piece of paper from the desk "What about a nice soap powder commercial, eh? All you've got to do is stick your hands in a bowl of suds. No dialogue, no nothing. Just your hands and a bowl of suds. What do you say?"

V: "But what's my motivation?"

W: "They're paying £300"

V: "I'll do it."

Wishaw gets up and escorts Veronica to the door

V: "If I bent down a little, perhaps I could…"

W: (*firmly*) "No V."

V: "I could scream a little? The water could be very hot…"

W: "Don't talk to me about hot water!   Just the hands, V. and think of the money"

49 Shades of...

The scene is set in the Menswear section of a department store. A very nondescript gentleman is wandering bemusedly around the various stands. A salesman approaches, optimistically:

Salesman: "Good morning sir, how are we today?"

Nondescript Gent: "I'm fine; I can't speak for you of course"

S: "I meant, sir, can I help you out at all"

NG: "I've only just come in!"

S: "Very droll, sir. Are you looking for anything in particular today?"

NG: "I was thinking about clothes"

S: "I think of little else, sir. Any particular garment at all? I have a rather nice houndstooth jacket that might take sir's fancy?" [*He plucks a sleeve from a rack*]

NG: "Oh no, that would be far too...definite. I'm hoping for something irredeemably tedious"

S: "Irredeemably tedious, really? I do have a beige pair of trousers that many have said are quite dull, would that be what sir had in mind?"

NG: "Beige? it's a bit...colourful, isn't it?"

S: "Oh, not these, sir." [*Flourishes a pair of very boring beige trousers from a nearby rack*] "No-one could ever accuse these of anything approaching colour."

NG: "They're a little...dramatic for my taste. If I was thinking of anything, I suppose I was thinking of grey."

S: "Grey? Yes, I suppose sir would be. How about this?" [*He produces a pair of smart, charcoal grey trousers*]

NG: [*shrinking back in horror*] "They're very...very grey, aren't they? Very definitely grey"

S: [*reproachfully*] "Sir did say he was thinking of grey"

NG: "Well, yes, but thinking of it and it coming at you like that, out of the...out of the..."

S: "Out of the grey, sir?"

NG   "Yes, yes, I suppose so. Well, it gave me a start, that's all"

S: "These are not to sir's taste?"

NG: "Have you anything that's not quite so definitely grey?"

S: [*dubiously*] "Not so definitely grey? Could sir perhaps give me some illustration of what he had in mind?"

NG: "Well, you know if you've washed a pair of white trousers with something black, by mistake, and the colour's run? That sort of thing."

S: "White trousers washed with black?" [*he muses for a moment*] "One moment, sir"

The salesman retires to a storeroom and there is the sound of packets being hurled about. Eventually he appears, with dishevelled hair but clutching a cellophane packet of trousers.

S: "These are from our Insipid collection. As you might imagine, it never really caught the imagination of the clothes-buying public and we now keep just a few items in stock for the, erm...discerning customer." [*He produces a pair of trousers of indeterminate greyness from the packet*] "Would these be the sort of thing that sir had in mind?"

NG: "Gosh, they really are rather dull, aren't they?"

S: "I think sir's term 'irredeemably tedious' rather sums it up"

NG: "Yes, yes, I think you're right. I almost forgot they were there, even while I was staring at them"

S: "I had much the same experience in the stock cupboard, sir. Shall I wrap them, or will sir wear them right now?"

NG: "Can you wrap them, please?" [*conspiratorially*] I rather want to delay the pleasure of wearing them until I get home."

S: [*moving swiftly to the cash register, with some relief*] "I quite understand. Will there be anything else, sir?"

NG: "I could do with a shirt to go with them. Do you have anything in off-white?"

S: [*placing his hands over both eyes and sighing dramatically*] "Off-white? Would sir mind if I enquired as to sir's occupation?"

NG: "

This is one of those occasions when I really couldn't come up with a nifty punchline, so I'm leaving it to you. If you can write a definitive ending to this sketch, email me at mail@philwhiteland.co.uk. There'll be a free book for the best submissions.

Thank you for taking the time to read these stories. Hope you enjoyed them! On the next few pages, you'll find a little more about me (as if you needed to know any more) and also details about the other books available via Amazon. You can always get in touch with me at

mail@philwhiteland.co.uk

Let me know if you would like to be informed of future publications.

Look forward to hearing from you.

Philip Whiteland, October, 2017.

About the Author

Philip is a retired university lecturer in Human Resource Management. You wouldn't believe how many potential friends he has lost, over the years, by telling them that. For much of his career he worked as a Human Resources Manager but he keeps that pretty quiet too.

He lives with his wife and cat on the edge of the Derbyshire Peak District or, as he says, more accurately just lives on the edge. Philip writes a monthly article for the Bygones section of the Derby Telegraph and is constantly trying out new pieces in his blog, The Slightly Odd World of Phil Whiteland.

If you're at a loose end, you can always follow Philip on Twitter @philwhiteland and on Facebook

Also by this Author

Steady Past Your Granny's

Steady Past Your Granny's

and other stories by
Philip Whiteland

Take a trip back to a different place and time. Where crowds of hunched and oddly dressed youths would probably be train-spotters, where you could have a reign of terror on a Sunday afternoon just by riding your cast-iron scooter across the blue brick pavement, and where the height of excitement on the street was getting two Beech Nut chewing gum packets on the fourth turn of the handle.

Philip Whiteland entertains with some keenly observed and very funny meanders through the past and present. Come and join him on the trip, but, whatever you do, remember to keep "Steady Past Your Granny's"

You can find "Steady Past Your Granny's" at:

http://getbook.at/Grannys

Crutches for Ducks

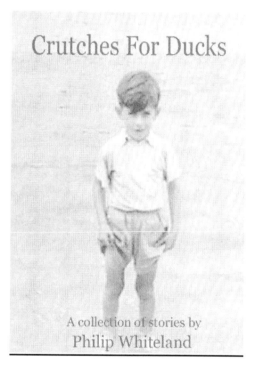

Crutches For Ducks

A collection of stories by
Philip Whiteland

Enter the slightly odd world of Phil Whiteland and slip back a few decades to a time when a John Bull Printing Outfit was the height of toy technology, when the telephone never stretched more than two feet from the front door, when every boy's knee was covered by a three inch square of brown sticking plaster and when a trolley-bus into town was a great adventure. This bumper collection of 'nostalgedy' stories (what happens when you mix nostalgia and comedy) coupled with some contemporary observations, guarantees a smile on every page and a chuckle in every chapter. Settle down for a step back in time and a giant leap forward in enjoyment, and if anyone asks you what you're doing, just tell them "Leos for meddlers..." (Complete with pictures - you have been warned!)

You can find "Crutches For Ducks" at:

http://getbook.at/crutchesforducks

A Kick at the Pantry Door

Philip Whiteland tickles your fancy (it's not a crime yet) once again with this compilation of stories, often with a food-based theme, from today and yesterday. Pull up a chair and tuck in! But first, a word from our Maitre d'Hotel:

"Welcome to the 'A Kick at the Pantry Door' restaurant. We have your favourite table ready and waiting and a selection of tasty and unusual dishes for your delectation and delight (but do bear in mind that the kitchen closes shortly as the Chef needs to go to his second job, rodding out blocked sewers). We have a few choice 'nostalgedy' stories for

Starters, some meatier ones for your Mains, a selection of 'curmudgeonly rants' or keen observations (you take your choice) for Dessert, and something unspeakable to go with your Coffee and Mints.

What are the ingredients? Well there's: Our dog's unfortunate addiction to railwaymen - avoiding the great outdoors - how not to take a picture - unfinished business in woodworking - entries as an indicator of intoxication - mowing under pressure - Easter as a moveable feast - a regrettable incident at the Crucifixion. You won't find any E numbers, dodgy additives or nuts in our meals, unless of course you count the Chef."

"Taking the interesting theme of the reader being a visitor to a restaurant, Philip sets out his book in a number of chapters under the headings of starters, main courses, desserts and coffee and mints. All the stories relate to his experiences growing up in Burton in the 1950s and 1960s...A flavour for the amusing content of the book is given in the first chapter, in which Philip recalls his childhood interest in eating dog biscuits." Derby Telegraph

You can find "A Kick at the Pantry Door" at:

http://getbook.at/AKickatthePantryDoor

Giving a Bull Strawberries

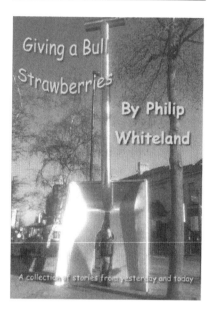

The fourth book in the ever popular 'nostalgedy' series of books. However, you don't need to start at Book 1 and work through to Book 4, or even start at Chapter 1 etc., you can dip in and out at will, and it will all make sense.

Yet another collection of tales from yesterday and today, designed to bring a smile to your lips (although I can't think of anywhere else you would want a smile) and a warm glow of recollection...wherever you fancy having a warm glow, I suppose.

They say that strategy is something that is only obvious in hindsight (I don't know who this 'they' is, but they seem to say a lot of things) but it is certainly true of this compilation. I was casting about for an overall theme for the stories when I realised that, one way or the other, the majority are about transport. Of course, I've now decided that this was my intention all along!

Armed with an overarching theme, the structure for the book just had to be after the style of the old Highway Code, which I remember poring over, first for my Cycling Proficiency Test and later for my Driving Test (and have never looked at it again since). Do you remember the old Highway Code? It used to have separate sections for the different road users, such as The Road User On Foot, The Road User On Two Wheels and so on. Well, if it was good enough for the Highway Code, it's definitely good enough for me. Hence this compilation is split into sections covering The Author on the Road, The Author on Rails, The Author at Sea and, finally, The Author at Large, which is a catch-all description of everything that I couldn't shoe-horn into the other three sections.

In these sections you will experience, amongst other things; the dubious delights of flat, warm beer at 08.30 in the morning as you set off by train for Blackpool, the horrifying sight of three less than agile people crossing the M5 on foot, the three-year slog of endeavouring to learn to drive and the trials of trying to find a working cash machine in Malaga in the wee small hours. All of these stories, and many more besides, are yours for the reading.

"Philip Whiteland brings his own special brand of nostalgic humour to a new book which has just been published. The fourth book in his amusing "nostalgedy" series, it carries the eye-catching title Giving a Bull Strawberries.

"It comprises a collection of tales from yesteryear and today and promises to bring a smile to people's lips along with a warm glow of recollection." Jane Goddard, Derby Telegraph

You can find "Giving A Bull Strawberries" at:http://getbook.at/BullStrawberries

A Christmas Cracker

A Christmas Cracker

A collection of seasonal stories

from

Philip Whiteland

Not really a 'nostalgedy' book, although it does contain some 'nostalgedy' pieces from the other books.

Are you ITCS yet? For those who don't know, we're talking about being In The Christmas Spirit here. Before you throw anything at your e-reader, just remember that this is a state of mind that advertisers and manufacturers try very hard to induce in you, and yet the answer is right here, in this little book. Being 'In The Christmas Spirit' is impossible to define. It's a bit like love, you know it when you're in it. Philip has gathered together a whole bunch of stories he's written about Christmases past and present, some factual, some fictional, over the years. Some of these, if you're a regular reader of his ramblings (and we know there are some of you out there...we can hear you breathing) you may recognise from previous collections, although updates have been made where it was sensible to do so. Interspersed with these familiar stories are others that have never previously seen the light of day, including a story featuring Josiah and Archibald, the two fictitious undertakers, written specifically for this collection. We really hope that you get as much enjoyment from reading these stories as we've had gathering them, and that you're ITCS before you can say "Ho, ho, ho!"

You can find "A Christmas Cracker" at:

http://mybook.to/xmascracker

Made in the USA
Lexington, KY
12 May 2018